THE FUTURE OF THEOLOGY

THE
FUTURE
OF
THEOLOGY

A philosophical basis
for contemporary Protestant thought

by FREDERICK SONTAG

THE WESTMINSTER PRESS · *Philadelphia*

The Scripture quotation from *The Jerusalem
Bible,* copyright © 1966 by Darton, Longman &
Todd, Ltd. and Doubleday & Company, Inc., is
used by permission.

STANDARD BOOK NO. 664–20848–7

LIBRARY OF CONGRESS CATALOG CARD NO. 68–21039

Published by The Westminster Press ®
Philadelphia, Pennsylvania

PRINTED IN THE UNITED STATES OF AMERICA

For
E. T. F. and A. L. F.

What is expected of stewards is that each one should be found worthy of his trust.

— I Corinthians 4:2
The Jerusalem Bible

PREFACE

ALL PURPOSIVE WRITING responds to some need, and this philosophical exploration into a basis for contemporary theology was occasioned by the unique invitation to lecture during 1966–1967 at the Pontifical College of S. Anselmo in Rome. So far as the record indicates, I was the first non-Catholic after Vatican II to be invited to offer regular courses in a Roman seminary. This volume stems from the lectures delivered there during the spring term to a seminar made up of theological students from a variety of institutions in Rome.

As the international college operated by the Benedictine congregations, S. Anselmo was itself helpful in shaping these lectures simply by allowing me to live there and to participate in the life of that community. The students in my seminar delivered prepared critiques on each of the chapters that follow. To their frankness this little book owes much of the credit for whatever clarity it now possesses. Daniel Day Williams, of Union Theological Seminary, read the entire draft of this essay with great care, and his numerous helpful suggestions for clarification have been incorporated. If the thesis of this essay can now be clearly understood, both the author and the reader owe him a debt of thanks. John Jensen also gave the manuscript a thorough reading and many of his suggestions were incorporated in the final version.

There are many more to whom this volume is also in-
debted. First of all, thanks are due to the Dan Murphy Foundation of Los Angeles for the grant that enabled me to accept
this pioneering invitation, which made it possible for my
family and me to spend a fantastic year in the Eternal City.
A special word of personal appreciation is due to Daniel
Donohue and the late Mrs. Donohue and to Richard Grant,
all of Los Angeles. Their interest and friendship have much
to do with whatever success this venture in Rome enjoyed.
His Eminence James Francis Cardinal McIntyre offered a
generous degree of ecumenical support. The Secretariat for
Christian Unity, and particularly His Eminence Augustin
Cardinal Bea, supported this appointment of a Protestant
philosopher to a Roman seminary. Pope Paul VI welcomed us
in a family audience. Calling me " a seeker after truth," he
welcomed us to Rome and greeted me " as a friend."

A former student and present friend, Fr. Paul Hale, Er.
Cam., first suggested that it might be possible to go to Rome
to teach. Fr. Hale's interest and the warm support of the
Prior and Benedictine Community at Valyermo, California,
have much to do with the fact that this philosophical venture
into theology ever came about in fact. The Sisters of Bethany,
those " angels in disguise " who operate Foyer Unitas in
Rome which offers hospitality to Protestants, quickly became our constant personal guides and friends. In word and
deed they teach the meaning of Christian love, and neither
I nor my family can imagine what our year would have been
like without these successors to the early Christians in Rome.

Vincent McAloon and the Notre Dame Center solved every
crisis for us. We came to depend on him for everything, from
insight into the warmth of the Italian people to locating the
typist, Mrs. Gloria DeLia, who did the original draft of this
essay for mimeographed distribution to my Roman students;
Mrs. Barbara Benton, of Claremont, California, typed the
final draft for publication. Admiral and Mrs. H. W. Ziroli
made life in Rome more homelike for strangers with the

warmth of their friendship and by their ability to communicate this friendship to others. As Congregationalists our home away from home in Rome was St. Paul's Within the Walls. As Episcopalians for the year we experienced ecumenism within Protestantism, and none of our family can forget the warmth and gentleness of Rev. Wilbur Woodham's reception.

Although at a later date I may try to do so, it really is not possible to put into words either the kindness of the Benedictine monks who welcomed me among them at S. Anselmo or all that I learned by this brief participation in their way of life. Gradually they took me into their confidence. The stories and conversations that they shared with me completely reformed my own ideas of the religious life. Because of the friendship of numerous individuals there, my outlook will happily never quite be the same again. Fr. Philip Edwards, O.S.B., gave me the assistance I needed in order to conduct a class under conditions that were very unlike my normal routine. My neighbor in the monastery at S. Anselmo, and now the lifelong friend of all the Sontag family, Fr. Stephen Keady, O.S.B., of Woodside Priory in California, did a thousand things a day for me. Without him life under the Roman seminary system would quickly have become impossible for this " separated brother." As Rector, Fr. Augustine Meyer, O.S.B., took the initiative in inviting me to Rome. As Rector pro tem, Fr. John Mueller, O.S.B., always responded to my needs, and the guest master and Dean of Theology, Fr. Gerard Bekes, O.S.B., welcomed me at meals. From all these men I learned the meaning of Benedictine hospitality.

The suggestion to give a series of lectures in Rome with this title was first made by my good friend Fr. Eleutherius Winance, O.S.B., of St. Andrew's Priory, Valyermo, California. Yet as this original idea developed, it grew into a much more general consideration of the whole contemporary scene, plus a call for a reexamination of and a new direction for American Protestant theology. As I worked in the midst of ancient Rome, these lectures increasingly took on " an American tone." I was forced to ask: What is the present state of theology in the United States, and what might American theology offer that either did not originate on the European Continent or does not now exist there in a developed form? Basically this means to ask: Can America find a way to give a unique approach to theology to others? It is the theme of this essay that to do this involves, first, a reexamination of philosophical premises and, then, the clear development of a philosophical basis conducive to such a novel contribution.

This volume does not carry out that task in detail. It is, instead, intentionally brief because a call to a new direction ought not to be confused with the detail of developing one particular suggestion. However, the attempt at new construction will be either haphazard or else not very novel unless a metaphysical questioning of both first principles and basic assumptions is first carried out. To this author, the contemporary theological scene seems to be most lacking, not in the detail of the discussion of issues, but both in the fundamental questioning of direction and in the formation of alternative philosophical bases for the development of theology.

In a different series of lectures at S. Anselmo in Rome, as well as in other writing begun and finished during that year, I started the detailed development of one new position. In a real sense, the following reexamination of the present philosophical and theological scene provides the basic orientation for this additional writing and for all future work projected by this author. Whatever new directions may result, this volume is offered to the prospective reader, not with the intent that it will either add scholarly detail to the literature on contemporary theology or be a new theology in itself, but simply in the hope that it may incite a new critique of basic principles and direction in the current theological scene in America. The development of the argument of this essay does not follow any standard current theological procedure, but then a call for a new style can only be in a new style itself, since it is the very basis of current approaches that is at issue. This " essay on the future " urges us not to accept but to call into question our current theological style and procedure. There are many signs that in Protestant theology " it is time for a change."

What I hope most of all is that these chapters will go somewhat " against the grain " of the trends in contemporary theology. Since the trial of Socrates, this has been the philosopher's ancient and contemporary task. Little fresh insight is to be gained by extending old premises farther, however comforting it is to know that one is a member of an already established movement. To incite intellectual rebellion — would that all students today saw this as their task. To try to turn thought into new ways is a more insecure undertaking, but occasionally it is also an immensely rewarding one.

F. S.

Claremont, California

CONTENTS

INTRODUCTION

IN ITS EARLY DAYS Protestantism could well afford to take its theological foundations for granted, since any protest will quite naturally receive its defining form from that against which it protests. This could not be otherwise, or else that reform movement would simply be something wholly new, and then it would not be a protest against that which it wished to oppose. There must be some basic similarity at least at the outset or else the objections cannot connect with their target. Once its original mission is accomplished, however, the protest movement must develop a *sui generis* basis or else it ceases to have a reason to exist.

In general, the original Protestant reform has been accomplished; in fact, today the reformed are reforming us! Thus, the necessity to form a genuine Protestant theology is now a matter that is crucial to the future existence of Protestantism. This present need would not be so difficult to meet if early Protestantism had not been antiphilosophical in its beginnings and if it had not communicated this aversion even down to the present day. Unfortunately, philosophy at the time of the Reformation probably deserved this theological rejection. What is even worse, the philosophy then current probably could not have provided a congenial basis for the renewed theology that the Reformers wanted so desperately to develop.

Whatever the situation at that time, there are two basic questions in our own day: (1) What philosophical forms have Protestants actually used recently in developing a theology? and (2) What forms might philosophy itself take in the present and in the future which could serve as a fruitful basis upon which to develop something distinctively Protestant in theology? If Protestants could actually develop new views, these might now be shared profitably with that original Roman Christian heritage from which we once separated ourselves in protest. Could this new philosophical basis be found for Protestantism today, it might actually promote greater unity among all Christians instead of simply deepening the sources of division. Why? Because we merely base our hopes on illusion if we think theology alone can provide the basis for any universal agreement.

Some ages have thought of philosophy and theology as synonymous, but we no longer share such confidence in the unifying power of verbal formulas. Thus, if Protestantism could now gain a clear theoretical basis of its own, while at the same time admitting that all theories need not and cannot be unified into one, then from a position of clarity and confidence Protestants might unite as individuals moved and touched by a common spirit. Theoretical differences need not always divide, but instead, if properly viewed, their very plurality can be accepted as a basis for agreement. From many theories, one spirit.

Until quite recently Protestantism has often appeared to take its philosophical basis for granted, and this has made it difficult to develop a philosophical framework purposefully, that is, to select its features for their theological utility. We have accepted the doctrine of historical and cultural determinism so completely that in both philosophy and theology we have simply tended to take our problems and develop them by whatever means we thought our times seemed to dictate. Under these circumstances we worked within a context as it was given to us, rather than feeling free to select from among the qualities and features of various philosophical theories. As a philosophical movement developed, it also seemed to dictate our theological response and to demand that our energies be devoted to it simply along the lines given to us.

If, however, we abandon the particular postulate that philosophical and theological views are given to us by our time and place, then the way in which questions arise would still distinguish the views of different eras from one another. In responding to these questions one would then be free from one's contemporary situation and be able to work out both a useful form of philosophy and an appropriate theological solution. With the exhaustion of the method of historical inquiry, we are now free to approach philosophy in a way that is not dictated to us by circumstances. Today, perhaps for the first time in centuries, we can ask the question without prejudice: What philosophical basis can we now develop for a Protestant theology?

To answer this does not mean simply to recount how known theological writers have been influenced by or have used what pieces of which philosophies. To be sure, that is part of the answer. Through a survey of that type, a perspective can be gained both on what the current alternatives are and, perhaps most importantly, on what might now be needed by way of balance and corrective. Yet both philosophy and theology are individual enterprises; they are not advanced a step merely by knowing what others in an era are doing. Such knowledge may be interesting, but, systematically speaking, it is still mostly a matter of professional curiosity and gossip.

Any new and useful philosophical form is born of some individual's slow selection, correction, and development of previous views. If that individual is successful in distilling for himself a view that is thoroughly his own, it may then become a form that others also find useful. Although many minds may come to see things in that one way too, a catalog listing of current individual trends is not productive of insight. It is only a guess as to the direction which a certain group might take next. To elaborate on current philosophical alternatives is not to try to influence existing groups or schools. Instead, such elaboration would offer a basis which some individual might then find useful for constructing his own theology — one which later might provide enlightenment to others also.

In the chapters that follow, three major themes are discussed at the same time, and the reader will see their relationship more clearly if he keeps these questions in mind as he proceeds:

1. The question of the relation of philosophy to theology, which is a universal problem in Christian thought.

2. The question of the possibility for a distinctively American approach to theology and the possible nature of such an American contribution.

3. The ecumenical question of the relationship of Protestant and Catholic theologies both historically and at the present time.

In this author's mind these three questions are tied together by the view that the philosophical basis needed for Protestant theology must be realistic, pluralistic, and open to new possibilities, and that these traits are all congenial to the American tradition and spirit. These are the themes and arguments that the reader is now invited to explore.

I *What kind of philosophy do we need?*

WERE PHILOSOPHY one and only one thing we could not ask what kind of philosophy we need, because the answer to this question would be ready-made. The fact that we do need to ask it indicates some uncertainty about philosophy itself and about the requirements for building a theology. Philosophy, of course, has never been all things to all men. Yet certain basic features concerning its area and its procedures remain distinctively the same, even if there must always be some flexibility in the way in which its principles are combined and its detail developed. If this were not true, the variety which actually characterizes philosophy's history would not make sense.

Theology is also uncertain about its exact philosophical requirements and it too must come to some basic understanding of itself before it can determine its relationship to philosophy and see clearly the manner in which it will incorporate, or exclude, philosophy in its development. It has traditionally been the case with philosophy that when the question of its theological involvement is raised, then its basic principles are challenged, uncovered, and defined in this process. For theology this is also true: To know its relationship to philosophy in general and to some particular form of it is to demand that it become clear about itself and about its processes and its purposes.

In this sense at least, no theology can afford the luxury of not determining itself in relation to philosophy. As it has always had the power to do, philosophy has the ability to reveal a discipline to be what it is. By contrast, and sometimes even by opposition, it forces any theology to reveal its premises, its assumptions, and its procedures. Given this perspective, the question, " What kind of philosophy does theology need? " can be answered by saying, " Any kind at all, whether positive or negative in its attitude." Although philosophy simply by its nature may perform this defining function, some of its forms are more helpful to theology than others. It is still true that we actually are given a limited range of choice for adoption and not the whole of philosophy. Of course, any theology must decide what kind of theology it intends to be before its specific needs in philosophy can become clear, so that the choice of philosophical method can at the same time reveal the special nature of that form of theology too.

There was a time when we expected philosophy to become a single system which would develop with certainty and finality. Had that been the case, then philosophy might have tyrannized over theology. Immanuel Kant, who fully believed that philosophy would develop in this way, was wise enough to place a limitation on philosophy. Thus, if it did not support theology, it was at least restricted from making final negative judgments on matters theological.

Philosophy and theology have now been bound together in this strange relationship for some time. Theology has either feared that philosophy would rule against it decisively and negatively or that it would simply take over and dictate whatever theological solutions it considered necessary. But philosophy has accepted its restricted realm, keeping away from theology while doubting its legitimacy. The same restriction that has kept philosophy out of the theological realm has also dictated that only within certain self-imposed limits of philosophy could the desired certainty and necessity be found.

A single, final, and necessary philosophy is rightly to be feared as tyrannical. Like the natural sciences, however, if philosophy does not hold to the idea of the necessity and singularity of any single theory, then it could support theology and not merely tyrannize over it. A speculative element would then be able to reappear in philosophy. Theology would become less alien to philosophy, and it would not need to attempt to develop its own kind of separate necessity in reaction to philosophy. Then the theological world would again have a flexibility of theory and could select from among metaphysical principles the one that fits its purposes best. There is, however, hardly a recent theology that has been offered in the spirit of knowing that there are acceptable alternatives to it. We are, then, placed in the position of being either completely for or against that theology, but this is a strange attitude which is alien to the true spirit of philosophy.

Philosophy can still be domineering when it accepts a certain evolutionary view and assumes that one and only one outlook can be adopted by " modern man." In such a case a philosophical view would be forced upon us without being required to justify its basic assumptions, as over against the other alternatives that are available. Then, for instance, a philosophical view can rule out the possibility of miracles without asking whether, under certain conditions, a framework that might permit miracles could be acceptable and on what ground.

When a philosophy dominates without having its metaphysical principles questioned, then all that will not fit its particular criteria is automatically ruled out. For example, miracles may be classed as " mythological " when, by another theory, they need not be thought of in that way at all. Philosophical outlooks that seem to accept without question a rigid view of science determine the limits of theology even before the issues can be discussed.

If an age simply by being what it is need not have a certain philosophical attitude, then a variety of metaphysical frameworks become available. All are not equally possible or usable without consideration, but at least the traditional metaphysical situation applies. That is, first principles must be justified by the one who uses them, instead of the restrictive belief that the time somehow dictates our basic outlook. The latter metaphysical belief borders on the vicious because it not only claims exclusive right to be true without exception but it holds these rights to be in no need of justification. However, when the goal and the method of philosophy become an open question, theology is not of necessity forced to any one conclusion; rather, it must justify each proposed solution on its own merits. In this situation no theoretical system can now take itself for granted as the sole possibility for that day.

If philosophy no longer sees itself as a parallel to mathematics and physics, or more precisely, if mathematics and physics no longer have a goal of singularity, finality, and necessity in theory, then philosophy is once more forced to be itself. Philosophy need not consider its own development as like in kind to the sciences, since it now does not seek to be simply one among them. Were the sciences theoretically able to achieve finality and necessity, then philosophy might be rendered superfluous (as some have supposed it is or will be), and theology would become even more dispensable.

When philosophy regains its rightful place, asking questions that no science can determine for it, it becomes less certain but also more flexible so that theology can once again utilize its support. Theology is in need of such philosophy because its basic principles and procedures are not fixed but must be worked out openly in the face of a variety of alternatives. This is the work of philosophy, not the rigid development of some one given set of theological procedures.

When theology becomes open and flexible, it needs to have philosophical alternatives in order to be able to determine its course freely, so that it does not merely become subject to some one philosophical prejudice. In this case it is more hazardous to theology's independence not to use philosophy than to do so, because if a fundamental critique of first principles is omitted, theology's course would simply be determined by some unexamined view. When theology does not seek this self-protective first philosophical step it risks not distinguishing itself clearly enough from religious belief and practice. For the one who accepts a set religious path and a particular given community, procedure may appear as a necessity and as not subject to argument. Of course, this is never the same as a theological question, which must be developed within a consciously stated context and has no binding power on any mind merely due to its relation to a religious tradition. Religious tradition may contain important statements, but it is not itself a conscious and a critical development of them.

Consider miracles and mythology. David Hume was right in thinking that nothing is impossible per se. Anything might happen next. The main questions are: which laws to accept, whether and under what conditions we can conceive of exceptions to them, whether a law itself can be suspended, and what the criteria are that we establish for belief. Hume is clear in admitting that he prefers to abide simply by the majority of common belief. Naturally, given these conditions, neither Hume nor Rudolf Bultmann can accept a miraculous event and be self-consistent. But laws and criteria are neither trees nor perceptions of sense, and thus they may vary in interpretation according to the basic framework that is adopted.

If one introduces a God as a principle himself responsible for laws, and if such a God is given any degree of freedom of choice, then the suspension of a law in any given instance for stated reasons is quite conceivable and rational. Nothing is in itself " mythological " or destined to be so from the event's first telling. An event may be " real " under one of several sets of criteria or " unreal " under any one of several others. If we abandon the assumption that existing at one point of time of itself imposes criteria upon our thought, then nothing but the stated operating principles can determine the reality or the unreality of events. The only error here would be not to realize this and to fail to state and to defend one's selection of criteria for " reality " as if this did not need to be done.

If one abandons the postulate that all sane men must think alike, then the natural scientist may find good reason, for his own purpose, not to admit exceptions to any law that is currently adopted. This, however, does not restrict the theologian from operating differently, nor does it require him to feel inferior in doing so. To protect himself from being dictated to by a particular philosophy in regard to the criteria of reality and unreality, the theologian ought first to function as a metaphysician, since the determination of criteria for evaluating reality is the metaphysician's primary task. That is why in an unmetaphysical age the theologian is unaided and is thus exposed, perhaps accepting his metaphysics without prior consideration. That is also why he is so much more liable to fall prey to unexamined metaphysical assumptions which may unavoidably distort his work.

What form of philosophy do we need? We repeat the original question, and now we can get a clearer answer: a philosophy that does not uncontrollably distort the Christian message, i.e., if the theology be Christian, because no theology can be drawn from a philosophy without some prior particular religious content. The theologian may, of course, decide independently to reject some portion of his tradition, such as the resurrection. It is his individual privilege to reach this decision on independent grounds if he is prepared to defend it openly, although his tradition may in turn decide not to follow him at all or only in part.

If the theologian decides that the external demands of some philosophical premise or set of premises requires him to alter his course, he is neglecting his function and he becomes a helpless victim of ideas. Obviously, going to the opposite extreme, making continued blind affirmations without an examination of alternatives is also a surrender to dogmatism. It may very well be the case that, in the process of testing various philosophical frameworks, he will also question earlier unexamined beliefs — which in itself is the very meaning of philosophy.

For a theologian to assume, however, that some one philosophy is dictated to him or to believe either that he has no philosophy or that his view is one without possible exception, that is the worst conceivable state for theology. As the theologian exercises, i.e., as he " works out " as a philosopher, he sees how assumptions change in perspective as different postulates are developed. He learns what some postulates allow and how others make it more difficult to accomplish his purpose. In this process theology grows and matures. Its hidden assumptions and problems rise to the surface, and then we learn what various philosophical postulates will do when applied to various problems. The content of religious belief is never exactly the same when it emerges from this procedure. If it were, it would not be worth going through the process of philosophical refinement. However, to think that we have no control over this development, or that it is one that we have an option to avoid, this is a blindness that philosophy tries to cure.

What kind of philosophy do we want? We ask the question again, and one answer that we now know we cannot accept is: a philosophy that will either require belief or guarantee answers with a necessity beyond doubt. We cannot expect philosophy to provide this rigidity in an applied situation, although that is what makes philosophy now safe for theological use. Some theologians, of course, may shy away from philosophy on just these grounds, i.e., that in raising questions, philosophy leaves whatever it touches always capable of doubt. If theologians find this quality undesirable for religion, they confuse the roles of philosophy, theology, and religion, or else they fail to understand that philosophy cannot prohibit a man from believing what he wants to, that is, if he is willing to defend it. Theology, it is true, can no more be absolute in its propositions than the philosophical postulates which it uses can be thought to be without alternative. Internally, each proposition can be affirmed as being firmly consistent with the basic assumptions, but ultimately each can be replaced by various alternatives.

A religious man need not be anxious about such an " if-then " quality invading his theology. That is, he should not fear philosophy if he properly understands how his religious belief differs from a theological elaboration of it and if he recognizes the independent personal roots from which his belief stems. Theological investigation may alter his religious convictions, it is true, but this need not be simply because some theology demands assent as being the only possible view open to an intelligent man. In fact, religious belief gains both strength and independence when theology abandons its claim to necessity because in that situation theology cannot be confused with religion.

Religious belief imitates God on the day of creation, in that it wills for itself one particular path which it then pledges to follow despite the alternative routes open to it. Theological alternatives reflect the possibilities from among which God elected our form of creation and the alternatives from among which he wills to sustain it. This is just how a man selects his religious belief. He gives it a form of definiteness which it could never have simply as one among all of the possible paths — if it were not within the power of his will to decide and to sustain that decision constantly.

" Freedom " is the major concept of our day, and theologically we should proceed with this in mind. For all too long theologians, while realizing their kinship to philosophy, have acted like men determined to think that some particular philosophy was required of them. Philosophers have also thought this true for themselves, but this is not true now and it is time that theology found it out. If as philosophers we have recently declared ourselves free from historical determinism, then theologians are free too. Their situation among alternative postulates is no better, and no worse, than that of any man in any theoretical field.

Because they are closer to fundamental questions, theologians ought to recognize the dependence of their answers upon certain basic assumptions. This, however, does not make them inferior to others whose rigor may have the appearance of finality within a particular context. Instead, the superiority of the theologian lies in becoming conscious of the dependent quality of his conclusions. He demonstrates his freedom by a knowing choice of his premises, and he proceeds more freely when he is not dominated by a feeling of finality that in the end will prove to be merely contextual.

The answer to the original question asked in this chapter is, "We want the kind of philosophy that we want." The meaning is, however, more technical and less arbitrary than this may sound. It is only arbitrary to choose a position without regard to criteria and to do so without reasons that can be explained. By contrast, "rationalization" is a more meaningful word, although it is sometimes associated with another abused word, "apology." Both words apply to the clarification, explanation, or the defense of the reasons for the principles or position selected. "Rationalization" and "apology" received their bad connotations as a result of a naïve and fantastic assumption that soon one and only one position and belief would be rationally defensible. If various alternatives are now admittedly open to use, apology today becomes a needed process to explain one's position rationally to those men with whom one differs. Clearly, the theologian must eventually attempt to discover what the philosophical requirements of his special theological goals are. Only then can he see if such a framework can be constructed and rendered acceptable to intelligence.

The virtue of philosophy has often been thought to lie in

its constantly critical viewpoint, one from whose inspection
no assumption is immune no matter how basic. In fact, the
more fundamental the unexamined belief the better it is as
far as philosophical scrutiny is concerned. For this reason,
theology has often feared philosophy, but in doing so, it sometimes overlooks the value of philosophy to theology at just
this point. Associated as it is with certain human beliefs, theology has a natural tendency to become ingrown in its
thoughts, particularly in the terms it uses and in the ways it
asks its questions. Philosophy, on the other hand, means to
develop a high degree of sensitivity to the meaning of terms,
knowing that the form of the expression is never neutral,
that the terms used will influence the conclusion, and that
the way in which the question is phrased is already half the
answer.

When any theology becomes ingrown and fails to reflect
on the alternatives to its particular form, it ought not to take
satisfaction in this easy situation, even if some group still
agrees to speak in those terms. By doing so, it loses its effec-
tiveness, not only for those others with whom it tries to communicate but eventually even for its devoted followers. The
doctrines become so familiar that the words lose their power
to incite the hearer either to radical thought or to action.
Unlike philosophy, theology cannot afford to be practiced
for its own sake. It has an ulterior purpose, i.e., to support and
clarify religious belief, which a philosophy may or may not
have.

Paradoxically, theology needs philosophy precisely because
philosophy offers the basic criticism that theology needs to
be sure that its doctrine stays alive as to its form. Otherwise,
it cannot attain through the vitality of its words a power over
both the minds and actions of its followers. If theological
thought loses contact, it cannot be effective as an outgoing
message, whatever its intramural advantages may be. Philosophy can be appraised as to its usefulness to theology here, i.e.,

to the extent philosophy can clarify a theology by providing it with a contrast to itself. Of course, there may be times when philosophy would simply block theological expression. However, without the constant goad of philosophical criticism, theology can become sluggish and content to work only where its basic premises are already accepted. A vital theology ought to be able to communicate its message to the listening unbeliever.

If the nineteenth century witnessed a great missionary outreach of Christianity, it seems clear that no comparable power invigorates theology in our time. In the next chapter we will examine the contemporary theological scene, but, whatever degree of vitality may be in theology today, it is clear that it does not have the power to reach out to the wide number of men who are outside its sphere. For the experts who formulate it, theology is a technical affair, but, even more than in the case of philosophy, the best theological views have been carried over into all areas of life. Our current religious activism, strangely enough, seems to be antitheological (in the sense of traditional theology) rather than to be flowing from a theology. In any case, the sensitivity to basic reformulation which philosophy can provide appears to be needed today in order to rouse theology to some new and powerful expression, that is, if we can find the kind or kinds of philosophy that can do this.

We do not want or need a philosophy that will simply lead us inevitably to a particularly Christian conclusion, as Hegel thought philosophy did. Yet certainly we do want a philosophical perspective that can at least allow Christian assertions to be possible. No one philosophy can do everything, of course, and it may be a current theological mistake to take hold of some particular philosophy too exclusively — a rather uncritical and unphilosophical thing to do. Thus, the kind of philosophy we need today may very well be eclectic. Existentialism, for instance, may be very good for certain theological purposes and poor for others (e.g., the doctrine of God) . To be eclectic is not necessarily to be un-philosophical. In fact, the selection and comparison of various philosophical forms is just exactly the kind of process from which a new form of philosophy usually arises.

II *What are the current trends in Protestant theology?*

WHAT IS THE PRESENT situation in American Protestant theology? To answer this question is the same as to ask, What sources are open to us for building a contemporary American theology? To use the word " American " is not necessarily to be provincial, for the fact is that every possible philosophical and theological trend is to be found here at present. In a later chapter we will ask whether a genuinely American Protestant theology is possible today. Now it is enough to note that one of the chief differences between Protestant thought in America and that of most of the countries on the Continent is that American thought, at least for the moment, has no identifiable national character. Each of the major countries of Europe seems to have a distinctive tradition and mode of approach: England in contrast with Germany, for example. In America, of course, there are followers of certain German schools of philosophy and theology, but every other Continental trend is also represented here by some advocate. This variety produces a complex situation that is far from being uniform or easily described.

We will attempt first a brief description of some of the many trends in current theology. In Chapter III we will describe the current situation in philosophy to see whether any available philosophical approaches can serve as a basis for a

contemporary Protestant theology. When later we examine
the possibility of building a distinctively American Protestant
theology, we will see that " diversity " will probably be its distinguishing characteristic.

Although no philosophy or theology can include every present or past theory (we have lost our faith in Hegel), still this
diversity, as contrasted with a " school " or a single tradition,
is the context in which American thought grows. While it is
true that any American can, of course, become a follower of
some theology or philosophy that is not necessarily American
in origin, it is also true that out of this diversity some distinctively American tradition might come. Heterodoxy then,
not chaos, is the primary characteristic of American Protestant theology.

What follows is not a definitive analysis of current theological schools and trends but rather an attempt to characterize
the movements of our time with an eye to appraising what
each tells us about the theological situation today.

1. The " radical theologians," who do not all form one
school, are almost too new a group to appraise, but it is important to ask what their appearance tells us about the
present theological scene. Interestingly enough, the attitude
taken by this group bears a striking resemblance to the liberal theology which developed in America in the last half of
the nineteenth century and which everyone thought had gone
with Karl Barth's coming. These radical theologians do not
aim at a new interpretation of orthodoxy, but at a basic revision which will bring Christianity into line with something
that they can believe. If it is true, much traditional doctrine
must be let go without an attempt to reinterpret it. These
radical theologians want to see what meaning can be salvaged
for their idea of Christianity after this peeling away of traditional beliefs. Rudolf Bultmann, as well as Paul Tillich
and Dietrich Bonhoeffer, is often quoted, but this new movement is more a radical rejection than a redefinition of tradition.

Since this new group focuses on the issue of God, it is interesting that Tillich's view of God is rejected, whereas it is hard to say that Bultmann had a detailed theory. This seems to point up the present inadequacy of our inherited thought on the nature of God, no matter what strength our recent theologies may have had in other areas. There are many issues to be resolved about the nature of God, and at least for this radical group no current view of God is adequate. Why don't they simply set out to build one for themselves? In a sense they have tried, but the question is, What kind of God do they see? Their attitude toward philosophy and metaphysics and systematic theology is such that they are prevented, on their own grounds, from doing much positive construction. We learn from the radical theologians to ask: What might supply a more adequate theological view of God?

2. Paul Tillich is one of the most important writers to consider today, if we are canvassing the current American theological scene primarily with an eye to the types of philosophical thought which shape it. Perhaps more than any other theologian, Tillich has been consciously and reflectively philosophical. He is always careful to work out the role that philosophy plays in his thought, and this fact is reflected in his appeal. Tillich's audience cuts across all fields. The one man most widely read today outside religious and theological circles is undoubtedly Tillich. In the sense that his thought has religious predispositions, it has been responsible for a widespread revival of interest in religion, or at least for an interest in the questions where his views are the most novel, as for example, a new definition of faith. Part of this stimulation, of course, is due to the element of existentialism in his doctrine.

What is Tillich's present influence on theology? He certainly is still widely read and increasingly so in Catholic circles. Yet no single successor has arisen to continue his work, and it is difficult to discern any widespread professional following that is consciously building on his systematic foundations. While Tillich seemed to have a difficult time putting his thought down into the final form of his *Systematic Theology,* his followers do not even seem able to begin systematic construction.

Much is being done in theology today, but it all has the overtone of " follow-up work," of a carrying out of strains, ideas, and programs which were proposed by a previous generation if not by a previous century. Even the radicals, as already noted, are a rebirth of an earlier liberal theology. When the younger generation seems content to be followers, this does not portend much excitement in new theological formation.

3. Of all the major figures in contemporary American theology, the two Niebuhrs are perhaps the only real natives. H. Richard Niebuhr is widely read and representative of American theology, but Reinhold Niebuhr is the more influential of the two. Reinhold Niebuhr admits to an early influence by Barth and dialectical theology, but there is a great difference between Niebuhr and Continental theology. There is a practical, political, and pragmatic side to Niebuhr that makes him of all the recent figures the most American in temper. Niebuhr once described himself to me as " not a theologian, but a man with a social concern and an interest in Christian ethics." Certainly Niebuhr's influence on theology has been tremendous; almost by himself he restored theological study to vitality in America and made it a concern outside of seminaries and churches. In contrast to the optimism of liberal theology, his view was based upon an awareness of human sin which induced a return to a more traditionally religious and Biblical view of man.

In spite of the impetus to theological study that Niebuhr aroused, no person or group today carries on his thought with the same attractiveness or vitality. We must ask, Is his work really a systematic theology or can it lead to one? We can say that Niebuhr was not philosophical in his approach, and it may be that without this systematic structure, his thought is not expandable but instead remains tied to its times and to its author. In spite of its vitality in its own day, it does not seem able to carry itself over to another generation or to form the basis for a systematic extension. While Niebuhr was sympathetic to traditional theology and to the institutional church, it is interesting to note that those who most advocate social concern as the focal point of religious expression are today often predisposed against the institutional church and hostile to traditional doctrine, if not also atheistic. Niebuhr was not metaphysical, but the following generation, all of whom share his social emphasis, are militantly antimetaphysical. This might indicate that, without a systematic core and a philosophical structure, no view based on " social concern " can be sure that it will sustain its influence. It is all too evident that the same secular concerns can spring up from quite different sources, perhaps even based on an outlook that is not traditionally Christian at all.

At this point, we should note the most striking fact about the current American theological scene. There simply has not been anyone of comparable stature to take the place of Tillich or Niebuhr. The current field is notably lacking in anyone who evidences their qualities of originality and of a sustained systematic thought that can point out a new direction. Were this lull in current theology less obvious, perhaps the radical theologians would not get so much attention. Radicalism seems even more sensational in a time that is creatively dull. Although the radicals often appeal to Tillich in some form, the examination of this phenomenon will have to be dealt with separately.[1]

4. Karl Barth's following in America could not be more different from Tillich's and Niebuhr's. Niebuhr aroused as much social concern outside the church as within, and Tillich attracted intellectual attention in non-Christian as well as in Christian circles. Barth's influence in America is also widespread, but direct acquaintance with his work is still primarily confined to professional theology students and to those

who are intently interested in institutional Christianity. Partly for this reason, Barth is perhaps the Protestant theologian most congenial to Roman Catholics, except perhaps to those Catholics influenced by existentialism who may find Tillich more provocative. This is not to say that Barth's impact has not been considerable. His influence on the teachers of theology is most important here, and through these teachers almost every contemporary theological student is introduced to Barth's theological view. His lack of both a popular audience and non-Christian appeal is easy to understand from a brief glance at his works. The sheer quantity of his works is enormous. The style is scholarly and exceedingly involved with references to all the theological literature and complicated with long footnotes. The question is, Will Barth's influence spread or diminish? No one in America has arisen as a powerful spokesman or follower of Barth largely because the orientation of his theology toward the institutional church limits its audience and makes it less accessible to the non-Christian world. Even its terms and its language assume a reader who is already within the traditional theological structure. This is not to criticize Barth, since it is part of his view that theology should be traditional, but it is important to note this in any attempt to assess his influence on the American scene. His outreach is limited by the kind of theology that he builds. It is not noted for its radical innovations, and thus it is unlikely to appeal to radicals as an acceptable alternative. It will take a long time to digest Barth's copious writings, which certainly do not lend themselves to simple summary or presentation and which are not friendly toward either philosophy or nontraditional modes of thought.

5. In considering Rudolf Bultmann, one must also consider the whole movement of " Biblical theology," since Bultmann is a New Testament scholar turned theologian. His theology comes out of his New Testament work, and it is hard to understand it apart from this. In fact, there are good reasons to say that Bultmann is not a full-scale theologian, since

he treats only certain Biblical themes and attempts to build a theology on this basis. It is somewhat ironical that Bultmann, the Biblical scholar, instead of being antiphilosophical, is outspoken about his philosophical dependence (upon the existentialist Martin Heidegger) and about his acceptance of modern thought, while on the other hand, Barth, the systematic theologian, is suspicious of philosophical intrusion.

Barth talks a great deal about God, and he does this in a day in which such direct discussion has not often characterized theology. However, his view of God is embedded in his approach through church dogmatics, which makes his God not very extractable for purposes of philosophical theology and apologetics. By contrast, Bultmann has little to say about God that is of a systematic nature. His focus centers on a reinterpretation of the Biblical message, which depends heavily on the philosophy that is used and particularly on the view of God that is employed.

Our principal question for Bultmann is: Can an adequate theology be built using the New Testament as a basis? Another answer we seek is the reason for the growing tendency to give theology this Biblical orientation. In giving any answer here, we must note that the radical theologians invoke Bultmann as they did Tillich, although they criticize him for trying to preserve a traditional belief which his philosophical assumptions will not allow or justify if strictly taken.

Bultmann's thought is much followed by a vigorous group of Biblical interpreters. When it is appealed to popularly, as by the radical theologians, it is to support their rejection of traditional theology. Just as it is obvious from the beginning what the Heideggerian approach will lead to theologically, so it seems likely that Biblical theology will only be able to offer something beyond Bultmann if it becomes critical of its philosophical assumptions and then revises them. Odd that a Biblically based theology should inspire atheism! Perhaps this tells us that (*a*) the base being used is really a philosophy and that (*b*) an adequate doctrine of God cannot come from the Bible alone.

6. Dietrich Bonhoeffer is a name on the lips of many a theological student these days, Catholic as well as Protestant. Like Ludwig Wittgenstein in philosophy, he did not write much, but (again like Wittgenstein) a cult of followers has grown up around his legend. In Bonhoeffer's case, this is partly due to his martyr's death. Bonhoeffer did not reject God; rather, he wanted to reconstruct the traditional view. Nevertheless, this has not been the primary emphasis that others have given to his thought. Rather, a radical involvement in the secular world and the necessity to communicate the Christian faith in a worldly way have been the themes of Bonhoeffer's followers. This has not and cannot lead to a systematic reconstruction of our concept of God. Instead, it tends more to an association with radical theology and toward a rejection of all traditional structure whether ecclesiastical or theological.

Bonhoeffer's influence is perhaps widest and most powerful in instilling a fervor for concrete action, which tends not to influence the construction of theology but to turn men away from such a task. Like Niebuhr, Bonhoeffer is a theologian only in a special sense, but whereas Niebuhr's thought led to a revival of traditional theological concepts, Bonhoeffer tends to inspire a rejection of the formalizing of theology in favor of radical action. Perhaps the pragmatic and activist strain in American thought accounts for Bonhoeffer's widespread influence, as with Niebuhr before him. His influence on theology proper (in the systematic sense) is another matter. His writings do not seem to lead to the technical development of a full theological view, not even in order to support his ethical recommendations for action. In that sense his thought is in danger of leading away from constructive theology rather than toward it.

7. Conservative theology, or " fundamentalism," can never be overlooked in America, so widespread is it and in some

senses so uniquely American. It has until recently been almost antitheological in the traditional sense, but today it is more and more vocal on the theological scene. It cannot be overlooked when, after all, the largest Protestant denominations often lean in this direction. Fundamentalism may have an antiphilosophical or even an anti-intellectual character, which may be why the conservative denominations have been so inactive on the theological scene until recently. Later we will ask if Protestantism is by nature antiphilosophical, but for the moment the important point to note is that fundamentalism has now become a force on the American theological scene. A great deal of this influence, it is true, has come in the form of Biblical studies, since the general movement of Biblical theology is very near the center of current theological interest, but that is where one would expect conservative theology to start.

As Protestantism has become intellectually sophisticated in America, often doing so by borrowing heavily from European sources, it has also become less specifically Protestant, increasingly secular and not very recognizably American. Conservative theology has a valuable role to play in reminding American theologians of their origins and perhaps even of their heritage. Most important, it can introduce an evangelical note, one that has tended to decrease as theology grew increasingly academic. It is no accident that the only preacher of real fame today is a conservative and that other prominent preachers are usually from the more orthodox traditions. The evangelical orientation of conservative theology provides a healthy contrast to a European-directed theology which tends to be a debate between professors and is neither particularly pastoral in its concern nor powerful in its outreach to unbelievers.

8." Process theology," developed under the influence of Alfred North Whitehead, has continued to grow in importance. Contemporary followers are still attempting to build a full-scale theology on its base, but as yet this is an unfinished project. In the current theological scene its most striking feature is its tendency to concentrate on outlining the nature of God, in contrast with the lack of interest in the metaphysical exploration of the divine nature by other contemporary theological approaches. However, the extension of this outline into a complete theological system still remains to be accomplished. Classical theories tend to be rejected as inadequate by this group, but if it could come to some kind of compromise with tradition, process theology might then be able to formulate a restatement that is not simply a rejection of tradition. Whatever its fruitfulness may be, it is inappropriate to call any movement inspired by Whitehead either new or American in origin.

9. The influence and the study of historical figures and sources cannot be underestimated in an account of present theological trends. Appraisals of the current situation often yield to the temptation to consider as influential only those current or recent writers whose works have achieved a clear form and who are recognized as distinctive enough to provoke debate. The eight groups outlined above are all of this distinctive type, but to consider only these is to miss perhaps the most important element of the current American theological scene. The number of classical sources that are immediately available to the theological student today is truly unique, and this fact is fantastically important. What characterizes the American scene particularly is the presence of every trend and classical source, whereas in other countries the range may not be so wide and usually only one or two views will dominate. Perhaps more than anything else this *universal scope of theological interests and sources characterizes the American scene today.*

This openness to and interest in every conceivable piece of theology in print may also have its drawbacks, but this issue will be taken up later. The translations into English and the printing of the primary sources in readily available editions is an editorial and publishing contribution itself worthy of a story. What will be done in theology with all these sources and potential influences remains to be seen, but the catholicity of the scope is undeniable and in itself is an important theological factor. Except for those we have imported, Americans tend to have no "schools" of theology, except perhaps this openness to the influence of every land and time (just as we were open to the cultures of the immigrants from every land who flooded to our shores). It is true that sometimes these historical sources tend to be taught from a fixed viewpoint, i.e., one that colors the doctrine under consideration and gives it a particular form. But at least in general, Americans seem able to read a historical work just for itself and to allow it to influence them — perhaps just because they have no preexisting structure in terms of which they can assimilate it from the start.

What, then, can we say to summarize and appraise these current trends in American Protestant theology? The main impression is that we are in *a lull after the storm*. Bonhoeffer is gone. Tillich, Barth, Bultmann, and Niebuhr were all born well before the turn of the century and had the peak of their influence a generation ago. One cannot say that their views are now disturbing the scene or upsetting old patterns. Rather, they are now themselves the established pillars. After such a generation of giants and of revolutions in direction, an extended calm is almost to be expected. It is hard to shift a direction while it is in a sense still new, and it takes time to digest the quantity of theological writing that the first part of this century produced.

If so much of today's theology may be described as being becalmed, the radical theologians, it is true, do not fit that description, but their storm is really only a little disturbance. Theirs is not so much a clear, new systematic direction as it is the revival of an old rebellion. Now their assertions are stripped of any attempted compromises with tradition. It is a philosophical premise now followed ruthlessly to its conclusion. It is not strange that open and honest Americans should have done this to the subtleties of Bultmann and Tillich.

Having no figures on the scene of equivalent stature to the Tillichs and the Niebuhrs, what can we anticipate for the future? The presence of the radicals tends to indicate that theology needs a new direction, one which is perhaps as much philosophical as theological, and that the current theological offerings still leave many unsatisfied. There must, of course, be some time of quiet in order to take in what has been produced theologically before any new sense of direction can come. With all of the primary sources and stimulations that are available, it might be a good sign that so many potential voices are silent. This does not mean that no writing is going on. Lack of a clear new orientation has never stopped the presses, but it is a fact that no new theological direction is evident.

We are busy following trends today, but one would find it difficult to say in what real sense any of these are new. Bonhoeffer, after all, died during World War II. On the whole, we are still pushing to their logical conclusion the new suggestions made at least a generation ago. Our theological project should be called " Operation Cleanup." This need not be negative, for, in exploring a previous suggestion, a new insight itself capable of changing that direction can be found. In fact, that probably is how the great theological innovations of the first part of our century got their start. Moreover, the availability and the use of such a wide variety of classical figures may in itself detach us from any current popular favorite. Reintroducing an old perspective can open a new direction to us by its contrast with the present day. That also is probably how some of last generation's new insights first came.

That systematic theology is not a popular pastime today, even for theological students, is not necessarily a bad sign. An age only needs a few to do a basic reconstruction of its foundations; yet it must be admitted that it is hard to find any potent basic ferment, however small, in the present day. Historical interest is not the same as systematic construction, and can even be an escape from it. Ecumenical concerns are everywhere, but that does not take the place of the clear working out of a theology, one that would give us a framework within which to discuss our differences. *Much activity, but little that is novel,* is the result that we are obliged to report from this inning of play.

Perhaps the two most serious problems noticeable in current theology are the following: (1) The church simply does not have either the missionary outreach or the persuasive power that it formerly had, specifically in relation to those who are outside of its community — it shies from conversion. (2) The present theological discussion often tends, on the one hand, to shun technical theology or, on the other hand, to use terms meaningful only to those already committed to its own discipline. Undoubtedly these problems are related. Persuasive preaching is not somehow the direct result of systematic theology, but before a man can speak to someone who is not basically in sympathy with him, he must first know clearly what he believes himself. In order to persuade, one must not only know what one believes but also be able to justify it by reference to one's first principles. Clarity is the result of a definite systematic formulation. If the gospel were clear in itself, its theological history would not have been so violent.

The phenomena of sudden bursts of missionary power that appear within Christianity from time to time are perhaps not directly correlated with productive theological eras. The current theological uncertainty, however, does seem to be related to our religious insecurity. To depreciate technical theological construction, and at the same time to press for immediate and practical involvement, is at best a temporary relief from a basic intellectual uncertainty, an uncertainty that could be dangerous if unchecked. Anyone may work for good causes, even in a secular city. This involvement is helpful to the Christian only if he understands how his practical concern flows directly from Christian conviction, and if he also understands how his good work is evidence of a quality definable as specifically Christian, in distinction from the activity of non-Christians who might be doing exactly the same good work. Without a live technical theology, Christianity may disappear into practical work and never reemerge with anything distinctively Christian about its basic beliefs.

The radical theologians demonstrate that technical discussion about God's nature has been seriously lacking. Niebuhr and Bultmann do not have much to say on this subject. Tillich's God has mystical qualities and is neither directly approachable nor directly describable. Barth has a more complete doctrine of God, but it does not seem to stand out clearly or to be characterizable simply in either technical or nontechnical terms. In any case, whatever the merits and the demerits of recent theologies on this subject, the result seems obvious. No concept of God has emerged with sufficient clarity or holding power to support the claims of Christianity, either to supply a strong basis on which to preach or to offer an appeal powerful enough to draw outsiders to it. Paradoxically, there is little today that would seem less the center of theological focus than the doctrine of God, and yet surely here is where the systematic core is to be either found or lost.

A basic cause of this situation is existential philosophy, although certain other philosophical views are deeply involved. The tendency of existential interest has been to restrict all direct metaphysical discussion and to focus instead on the self or on its activity. Theology's present state, then, may actually be dependent upon the climate created for it by the dominant philosophical views. If certain projects are necessary for theology, such as the discussion of God's nature, these must at least be possible philosophically. If important issues cannot be discussed philosophically, then these necessities cannot be provided by theology. Thus it may very well be that, however philosophical or antiphilosophical current theologies are, the present situation may be more understandable in the light of the dominant philosophies than on the basis of the theological questions that supposedly are at the forefront of the discussion. It is not an accident that the radical theologians often appeal to British analytic thought, but we need to survey the present philosophical scene in order to see these implications more fully.

III *What philosophical sources are available?*

AN EXCELLENT RESPONSE to the question of this chapter is provided by John Macquarrie's comprehensive book *Twentieth-Century Religious Thought: The Frontiers of Philosophy and Theology, 1900–1960* (Harper & Row, Publishers, Inc., 1963). It is hard to think of any major philosopher who is left out of this account, so that this gives us a good perspective on the variety actually available today. However, we must not forget that Macquarrie has omitted the classical and the historical sources, and those can still play a large role as a base for any theological construction. Despite this *important reservation,* we can ask what major philosophical sources are affecting theology today, and what orientation these can provide in attempting to work out a new basis for a contemporary Protestant theology.

Macquarrie's account can also produce a needed lesson, a chastening reminder of how quickly philosophical fashions change and of how short a time it can take radical revolutions in thought to occur. Many, if not most, of the men listed are no longer either read or influential. This does not mean that current popularity is the only test. A writer who happens not to be read now can become a vital source at a later time. Although any theology must draw on the philosophy of its day, Macquarrie's book reminds us that a theology courts quick irrelevance if it simply accepts uncritically whatever philosophy happens to be current.

Macquarrie's *Twentieth-Century Religious Thought* presents a vast kaleidoscope in a clear statement, but the picture is still too varied and too exhaustive to be very helpful systematically. This chapter will attempt to focus briefly on certain views, those which emerge as potentially the most important for theological purposes, and to focus a critical and constructive eye on their potential theological fruitfulness.

1. *Existentialism* of all recent philosophical movements has had perhaps the greatest single impact on Protestant theology. This is not an easy phenomenon to assess since it includes many diverse figures. Moreover, in spite of its religious origins, it has led to atheism as well as to new meaning for religious concepts. Its importance for theology stems primarily from the fact that in recent times existentialism has been almost alone in linking together religious and philosophical interests. This is, however, a mixed blessing because many philosophers precisely for that reason have tended to reject existentialism. Yet it is plain that as a philosophy it has probably had a more widespread influence outside of professional circles than any other movement in recent centuries. For the first time in years, material has been produced that is of interest both to theology and to philosophy, not to mention the movement's vast literary influence.

Yet the breach between philosophy and theology has not yet been healed. This is partly because many philosophers refuse to recognize existentialism and partly because theological circles are cautious due to the atheistic tendency of existentialism. The ability of existentialism to give new meaning to the life of religious struggle is perhaps its chief asset. However, sometimes existentialism displays an antirationalistic strain that is hard on philosophy and an antisystematic bent that makes it difficult to use for a full-scale theological construction. Existentialism arose as a reaction against a certain philosophy and situation: Hegelianism and the passing of an aristocratic culture. It loses much of its meaning and its definite form when that against which it rebelled no longer exists and when, irony of ironies, it is no longer a radical minority but itself an orthodoxy and when it is no longer a matter of inner disposition but of outer revolt.

2. *Phenomenology* in its current form often comes mixed with existentialist thought, although its originator, Edmund Husserl, certainly did not intend it to be. Husserl wanted the same kind of rational certainty and scientific completeness that Hegelians did, which is what the existentialists revolted against. Jean-Paul Sartre and Martin Heidegger are by no means pure existentialists in the Kierkegaardian sense. Perhaps they can both be better understood if one sees their work as an attempt to build a system in the phenomenological mode (following Kant, not Hegel), combining this with a Kierkegaardian inspired radical psychology and a strong sense of the individual. Kierkegaard denied both system and certainty but phenomenology does not. In recent times these two supposedly divergent strains have formed some interesting blends.

In the strictest sense, however, phenomenology excludes classical metaphysics. It begins with human understanding and restricts any direct consideration of God except insofar as he may enter human consciousness. As far as theology is concerned phenomenology seems to center its attention on religious consciousness and not on God. Phenomenology's demand for certainty and finality perhaps prevents it from extending itself to the more uncertain material of God. It first limited itself to phenomena in the hope that it could achieve certainty by its very method. Therefore, for phenomenology to turn either to the unconscious in man or to a direct description of God would mean it would be forced to give up its self-imposed restrictions and perhaps involve itself in uncertainty again, thus defeating its own goal The problem of method, not metaphysical first principles, always remains phenomenology's first consideration, since it is important to

decide whether one thinks one can arrive at certain knowledge of a thing's nature from its description. God is a particularly difficult subject for this approach, since he seldom
appears in any immediate phenomena and then seldom to
more than a single individual.

3. *Process philosophy* is almost alone in its field in attempting a new theory of God's nature based on a realistic metaphysics, i.e., a belief in man's ability to grasp and state the
nature of things directly. Whitehead is perhaps the originator
of this view in recent times, although Henri Bergson's
thought leads in the same direction and has also been applied
to yield a theory of God. Neither man has a detailed description of God's nature, so an extension of their original views
has been required. Charles Hartshorne can be seen as doing
this for Whitehead, and Teilhard de Chardin for Bergson,
although other elements are also important in their thought.
Certain views on evolution are involved in this philosophy,
and this means that previous theories are not necessarily continued; more innovation in terminology and less interest in
classic formulations is required. Hence there is more difficulty in asking a God like this to answer the traditional
questions.

Perhaps the most significant feature of process philosophy,
however, is that it often leads to a limited God; thus the traditional assertion of God's omnipotence is denied from the
first. In any view of process, it is likely that God will become a
principle second to the idea of process itself. A greater value
tends to be set on novelty, freedom, and flexibility than on
tradition. In contrast to traditional theories, it seems that
God must not be all-powerful but only one element in the
process in order to preserve the goals of novelty. Most significant is the absence, so far, of a complete description of
God in these terms and a lack of development on this basis of
the implications for all the traditional theological questions.
Process philosophy promises a more full-scale revision in contemporary theology than it has yet been able to accomplish.

4. In the current situation perhaps nothing is more strange than the attempted use of *British analytic philosophy* for theological purposes. However, before listing its limitations for theological use, it is important to note its assets and virtues, which may make its influence in theology a lasting one. Most striking is its nonhistorical orientation. Existentialism, when it is combined with analytic philosophy (strange allies!), works to redirect philosophy quite radically away from its almost exclusive preoccupation with history. Existentialism in theology, however, as antihistorical as it is, still seems to get caught up in a continued stress upon the historical consciousness as it is used by theology. Perhaps only a far less sympathetic analytic philosophy can set theology free to discuss issues in a contemporary and systematic way.

Analysis is not antimetaphysical in the way logical positivism was. It has actually sparked a cautious metaphysical revival that might be helpful to theology, which has been for so long deprived of any metaphysical support from philosophy. Yet here the danger begins because analysis, at least as it follows after Wittgenstein, is dogmatic in its metaphysics and seems almost unable to allow for other viewpoints on philosophy. If its flat metaphysical assertions are questioned, however, this dogmatism might begin to lessen.

Analytic philosophy is very careful in its investigation of the technical meaning of terms. This has always characterized the philosophical temper, but perhaps analysis can again teach theology to pay attention to clear definition, an absolute prerequisite for building any contemporary constructive theology. Still, it tends to be antisystematic in its form, and theology needs a framework that can allow systematic formulation. Most important, analysis does not seem useful for making any constructive effort to delineate the divine nature. Its mode of procedure thus appears to be set against theology's greatest current need.

Analytic philosophy does not aim to establish new theories, and this is perhaps what we need most of all. Instead, it concentrates on the analysis of existing statements. Analytic thought tends to depend on current ideas in philosophy for its material, whereas theology needs more philosophical resources, both to enable it to generate new theories and to connect it to the tradition that has shaped its questions. Analytic thought shows some signs of extending itself into all forms of philosophy. This permissiveness could be good for theology, but then analysis would lose, even for theology, its distinctiveness as a philosophic approach with a single sharp focus.

5. In any appraisal of the current philosophical scene, as far as it relates to the needs of theology, the influence most likely to be overlooked is the role of *historical* (i.e., traditional) *theories*. Theology need only fear for its vitality when it becomes too dependent on the current situation for its philosophical forms. Philosophy also needs traditional sources for its health, but they are not as crucial to its life as they are to theology's. It is possible for philosophy to be almost completely contemporary; for instance, in the sense that both analysis and phenomenology are antihistorical in methodology. Theology has a stronger need for traditional questions, if not for traditional forms, in order to give its answers. It also needs metaphysics for its doctrine of God, which is something not every philosophical form has the nerve to provide.

The contemporary theologian does not have open to him only the current philosophies that are in vogue. In addition, every traditional theory is equally a potential source. Aristotle was not a contemporary of Thomas Aquinas, and yet he was helpful to the "Angelic Doctor." The sources that Aquinas quoted came from both the recent and the far past. In fact, some use of the classic forms of philosophy can provide the leverage that is often needed to free the theologian from the dominance of some one contemporary view. He need not be dominated by an exclusively classical approach, but at least the awareness of tradition can give him a sense of balance in eras other than his own and a perspective from which to judge present trends without falling victim to them.

6. In relatively recent times an almost exclusively *ethical approach* to theology has been suggested, probably most forcefully by Kant. In this approach, theology tends to become ethics or at least it is given an ethical base. Because of the link with Kantian sources, epistemology and methodology are its primary concerns rather than metaphysics. It is noteworthy that there was a time when " Christian ethics " was viewed as somehow capable of replacing traditional theology, but that time seems largely to have passed. Basic theological questions have now been revived and the nature of God is even admitted to be the central question.

An ethical approach tends to take the nature of its God for granted. Kant did not see the need to revise the traditional concept of God, but the radical theologians have at least put that alternative behind us. Either we rethink our concept of the nature of God now or else we will not have a God left to base an ethical theory upon. When God is assumed, ethics can appear to be the first question. When God is challenged, however, we can readily see that ethics depends on the prior formulation of an acceptable concept of God.

Whenever methodology and theory of knowledge seem to be the first questions for theology, the crucial task of constructing a theory of the divine nature may never be reached. Theology must certainly have a methodology that allows God to be considered, as well as a theory of knowledge that will support statements about God. However, both of these are worked out in conjunction with the development of a theory of the divine nature and not apart from or prior to it. Whatever else theology selects in appraising its philosophical base, it should demand a method of approach that does not allow its existing concepts of God to be neglected, since it is precisely these concepts that will tend to deteriorate if they are not reworked. We are now at the close of an epistemologically obsessed era and the resulting loss of reality in our concepts of God and of our ability to speak about him systematically should be all too evident today.

7. In Macquarrie's book the once-powerful movements of *idealism and pragmatism* appear to be almost totally lacking in present theological influence. These views have also faded relatively rapidly from the philosophical scene. Idealism almost dominated theology a generation ago, and, in a more limited way, pragmatism once molded much philosophical thought in America, particularly through William James and John Dewey. Of course, recent movements which have been so powerful are not likely to pass immediately without leaving a trace.

Both phenomenology and British analysis (not to mention existentialism) show a remarkable similarity to idealism in their stress upon the " self " and in their insistence upon the necessity to begin with the self's knowledge of itself. Because of religion's natural interest in the self, any view that concentrates on this aspect will tend to make religion and its problems meaningful. In this sense, idealism always provides a good theological context, but if it centers its attention entirely upon the human self without the metaphysical extension which Hegel gave it, idealism can block any consideration of God. Philosophically, this consequence can be accepted, but theologically it leads to the death of an already neglected theory of God.

Pragmatism is still forceful today in theology's natural tendency toward activism and in its shunning of theoretical abstractions. Pragmatism shows itself in theology's insistence that it is best worked out in the midst of practical action rather than in systematic thought. Thus, there seems to be some basis for a natural kinship between theology and pragmatic first principles. Pragmatism keeps religion meaningful by placing it in concrete situations that demand action. But if it blocks further metaphysical consideration, any theology based on pragmatism may find that the very God who at first seemed to demand the action can no longer be thought about with any degree of clarity.

8. *The philosophy of history and culture, the sociology and psychology of religion, comparative religion, and the history of religion* are all philosophical subjects from which theology can be evolved. They are all philosophical in context, insofar as there exist within each area important assumptions and questions about how and why a religion should be approached and a theology constructed in that way. That none of these studies were existent before the rise of modern philosophy attests to their underlying philosophical basis. A new philosophical view must have suggested each discipline as a context in which to investigate theology. Thus, it is important to look back to see what original assumptions were made in proposing to pursue theology in this way and to see whether these philosophies can still be accepted and justified. In philosophy, as in history, any revolution once accomplished tends to be accepted on principle without demanding the same examination of principles with which it first began.

Perhaps it is important for theological purposes to ask whether some particular evolutionary scheme is assumed in these philosophical approaches. Evolution in some very general sense may be an accepted fact in our age, but no one theory about it is final or needs to be taken for granted. And even if evolutionary theory is applicable in some area or areas, it need not apply to theology in any similar fashion.

In any case, before that problem can be decided, it is necessary to find out what theology is, since to assume some one definition of the theological enterprise is dangerous. To do this requires a critical, challenging examination of principles once agreed on for procedure and definitions. Thus theology needs philosophy, since such root investigation is precisely philosophy's task. Otherwise, theology may fall victim to some now concealed metaphysical assumption.

What philosophical sources are now available? Do these eight philosophical approaches, either singly or all together or in some combination supply the answer, or are there sources other than these? At least we know that more than one alternative is available to theology; no theologian must feel that he has to accept only one philosophical form or else reject all of philosophy. This is perhaps our most important conclusion, for theology tends to fear philosophy only when it thinks that theology's questions and answers will be forced into some one form against its will. As long as a variety of philosophies are available, the theologian is a free agent. Perhaps he is not completely free to reject all philosophy, but at least he is free to test and to select a view that seems compatible with and conducive to his goal. Of course, that is not the end of the matter but only the beginning. The theologian must justify his choice in the process of working out his detailed theories, but at least now he knows that he need not be the victim of some single philosophical view.

Probably no theologian has ever taken over ready-made a single whole system of philosophy. If he had, it would not speak well for his awareness of the consequences of adhering to any one viewpoint. Any constructive process must be selective and eclectic, since the forming of a new view requires the reinterpretation of some of the substantive ingredients. Uncritical minds may automatically shape certain problems or statements to fit into one system of expression, but the theologian must be powerful enough in his theoretical training to select appropriate philosophical instruments and to mold them in the process of his consideration.

What can be said by way of summary concerning the present situation after this admittedly brief listing of the available philosophical sources? By way of answer, another question must be asked first: Do we actually have available today exactly the same variety of philosophical sources that have been available in any age? In recent times we have tended to assume either a historical contextualism or some form of evolution, and so it has seemed that past theories were no longer available to us and that we were restricted to the use of dominant or new trends. The first impression one has on reading Macquarrie's account of religious thought in the twentieth century is how much wider and more extensive the current variety is than might have been supposed. The second impression one has on examining the thought of the recent past is that almost every variety of thought that has been present in any other age is also being redeveloped somewhere today.

Sometimes we are fooled by superficial change or terminological novelty, but beneath the surface the same general span of philosophical views is available. This is particularly true if we keep in mind the relevance of historical sources (category 5 above). Some views may be more actively explored and expanded at any given time, but as long as historical texts are available, the total range of views that they present may be considered. In fact, it may very well be that the insight provided by reading some historical author will spark the formation of a modern theory. The net result of our survey is to show that almost every philosophical form is perpetually available for development, unless the age is distorted. If he revives certain theories, a man may have to count on moving against a popular trend, but almost every approach offers a contemporary possibility. Traditional theories cannot be appropriated just as they were formulated, but they are there and can be modified to serve a new age.

Elsewhere, I have developed the view that it may not be possible to approach any theory in the present or past without altering it. Theories are not things; a mind cannot grasp a theory immediately or exactly in its original form. Words themselves are so changeable a medium that each inherited philosophical doctrine is modified as it is handed down by each mind that reads it. Mathematics can pass on a theory more accurately than language can. In this sense every theory, whether past or contemporary, provides certain new materials for a contemporary interpretation, although this interpretation is never the single, definitive, and complete view.

If he sees philosophy in these terms, a philosopher in any age may have the same elements before him, although as he approaches their variety and combination the detail of their specific form may be changed.

One false impression that might have arisen as a result of listing the eight contemporary sources above may need to be corrected. Although there is some justification for the tendency to think in terms of " schools," the most influential sources are less often derived from a particular school than from the work of one man, and perhaps not even from his work as a whole but from just one book or section of one. Individual thinkers can probably be grouped according to similarities, but their contribution and their influence as a philosophical source comes from them primarily as individuals, not as representatives of a school. New thought seems to be opened up, not by the acceptance of the general structure of some recognized type of doctrine, but by the fresh insights that a talented man can derive from reexamining these doctrines and then recording these special insights. The unique qualities that a man adds to an already known general view make him distinctive and inspirational to other readers.

Which of the eight sources listed above seems to have been most influential today and in the recent past as far as Protestant theological formation goes? Existentialism (1) is so widespread that it hardly requires further mention. Perhaps for the first time since the Reformation, we have in it a philosophy that is at once a blend of religion and theology; even in its atheistic forms it raises meaningful questions and offers sympathetic attitudes. Tillich and Heidegger are probably the two outstanding men who have used existentialist materials to form a fruitful mode of thought. Due to its orientation, existentialism tends to be strong on anthropology and, at best, weak on ontology and a doctrine of God. Heidegger, of course, also belongs to the phenomenological movement (2). Where the analysis of the religious consciousness is our primary concern, phenomenology's particular methodology seems appropriate.

Among those who approach theology metaphysically process philosophy (3) is perhaps strongest. Although it has not
yet produced a full-scale metaphysical theology, it does at
least provide a set of concepts in terms of which God may
once again be thought about, in new ways as well as old.
British analysis (4) is currently being explored as a theological methodology. Yet, perhaps in keeping with its principles, it has produced no full-scale revision of theology, but instead has clarified individual questions by a new approach.
The availability, the usefulness, and the influence of all the
material left by historical figures (5) are so pronounced that
the strength of this source is probably the most difficult of
all to appraise. Hardly any contemporary work fails to include or to build upon some selection of historical doctrines.

The other contemporary philosophical sources, in descend-
ing order, seem less influential at the present, although a short
time ago this was not the case. This indicates the rapid shift
that takes place between succeeding philosophical moods.
The ethical approach (6) must always have some place of
importance, since religious doctrine by nature has ethical
content. Perhaps the increasing feeling that we are losing our
a priori ethical intuitions, to speak in the Kantian fashion,
has made an ethical approach to philosophy seem less possible in the present day. In a stable era, when fundamental
values are not under basic challenge, ethics can appear to be
a solid and immediate approach to theology. Today we seem
to feel the need to work out more fundamental questions
before we can rely on ethics as a basic approach.

Once idealism and pragmatism (7) held sway over America and England and the Continent, but now it is hard to
attribute much direct theological influence to either source.
We will explore later how pragmatism might help to form an
"American theology," but for the present little theological
inspiration seems to come from either of these philosophies.
On the other hand, the philosophies of history and culture,

and the others (8) still seem very dominant in their hold upon theological forms of expression. The categories that are characteristic of these approaches continue to be used everywhere in theology, although there are many signs that the metaphysics behind them is under challenge. British analysis, existentialism, and radical theology are all challenges to these historical and cultural philosophies. A major shift in theological methodology, approach, and terminology may already be under way.

At various points throughout his book, and in its conclusion, Macquarrie makes certain critical remarks about the twentieth-century views that he presents.[2] It would be well to examine these remarks here to see if they indicate how the various philosophical sources can be used in contemporary theological construction. One of the first things Macquarrie notes is that "our way of looking at things has changed" (p. 19). He thinks we have lost a certain pervasive note of optimism, a quality which was characteristic at the turn of the century. Be that as it may, for our purposes two factors are important: (1) We should be careful about assuming that we have simply passed from one mode of thought, which told us how theology must be written, on to another mode, which similarly dictates our philosophical framework, whatever it may be. (2) We should be aware that what we actually see now is not a dialectical progression from one mode to another but an opening to every mode of philosophy, whether past or present. This expansion of sources — and the freedom that it offers from the domination of any one "school" — is perhaps the most important single change for theology today.

Macquarrie thinks that this change may be connected to a decline of belief in evolution and progress as dominant philosophical theories. He also discerns a shift from the notion of "substance" (p. 20) to more dynamic concepts such as "process" (p. 21). We must not assume that such an emphasis on different categories for interpretation is somehow a necessity to theology in our age. What has happened is that process philosophy has been added to the great variety of philosophical forms now available. Macquarrie also sees a loss of interest in comprehensiveness (p. 21) as well as a separation between philosophy and theology, although earlier in the century most philosophers gave some attention to religion. This may be true, but the question is, Do we need to correct this situation?

We must conclude, from where we seem to stand today, that theology ought to establish its own use of philosophy. Yet, given the separation between the two, we must first appraise the fruitfulness of any philosophical form for theological purposes. An analysis must be made of any hostility to theology that might be inherent in a philosopher's basic assumptions, although that philosopher might be right. Unless a philosophy shows any obvious and built-in theological interest, the use of any contemporary philosophical view must be preceded by an attempt to estimate how its basic assumptions might either clarify theology or frustrate its aims. If a single philosophical form was dictated to us by our age, we might not have this liberty. If an inspection of our era reveals a multiplicity of sources, the theologian is free to pick his philosophy openly, of course with an eye to the advantages and disadvantages and perhaps by using parts of several views.

Certain forms of a basic naturalistic outlook are widespread today, but so too are spiritualistic or idealistic (perhaps better, " metaphysical ") forms of philosophy (p. 22). Noting this, one must ask the question: Despite new formulations and terminologies, are these not the same basic divisions in philosophical views that we have always faced, admitting that at various times one outlook might be more dominant or popular than the other? If we grant that neither basic outlook has succeeded in excluding the other completely and that an irreducible variety of sources is a permanent condition that defines philosophy, theology would seem to have freedom in its philosophical choice. Only the belief that a certain philosophical outlook must dominate the opinion of a given age could deny the theologian his freedom, but that belief is an assumption we know can and must be challenged.

Macquarrie clearly sees that the now declining philosophy of idealism has theological advantages because it is basically metaphysical in outlook and method (p. 42). This seems to indicate not only that theology needs metaphysics but that theology should be on the alert whenever metaphysics is inhibited or restricted. If theological questions are related to metaphysical issues in any way, then any restriction of metaphysics inhibits theological development as well. With a variety of sources open to it, no theology needs to use an antimetaphysical basis unless it wants to, since no one metaphysical approach is forced upon it.

In considering ethically based religious views (pp. 92–94), Macquarrie shows how these tend to work against transcendental beliefs; the prospective theologian should be aware that an ethical approach may be antimetaphysical and that it can work against philosophical discussion of God. For theology to be denied a philosophical basis to explore the divine nature is a serious deprivation, and since at least some philosophies will allow this exploration the theologian should know that he can have his choice in this matter.

Naturalistic philosophies, as Macquarrie points out (pp. 111–115), tend to see philosophy as aiming toward the early model of science, i.e., as a fixed set of conclusions universally agreed upon. Not only is this not the only way in which philosophy (or science) can be defined, but such views of philosophy involve assumptions which are unnecessary and which may be doubted. A theologian therefore cannot approach these naturalistic views without first asking some very serious questions about the very nature of philosophy and science.

Now that no one philosophy is determined for us, we can approach any philosophy only after engaging in that most primary of philosophical inquiry: What is philosophy and what is its basis? Since philosophy is not a single system of thought, theology may reject any given philosophical view without rejecting all of philosophy. After examining this primary question, theology must next determine that philosophy's aim. If any theory of philosophy would restrict his own goals too severely, the theologian must question its usefulness for his purposes. Comprehensiveness, at least to some degree, seems to be a theological need, so one basic theological task is to consider the arguments that would either limit philosophy or else restrict its application.

It is perhaps most necessary to clarify the philosophical basis upon which the historical, cultural, and sociological approaches to religion rest. Macquarrie makes clear that these approaches to religion may rule out others or even make a technical theology impossible (pp. 136, 152, 166). For theology to discuss these issues would, therefore, seem to be a matter of some importance.

This is particularly true where the historical approach is concerned, since recent theology almost seems to be divided between those who assume, sometimes uncritically, that this is *the mode* for theology and those who reject it flatly.

The comparative study of various philosophies involves us in metaphysics, because the uncovering and critical appraisal of basic assumptions is precisely the primary task of metaphysics, whether or not it moves on to other more constructive work. A theologian must engage in philosophy before he can either accept one philosophy or reject all philosophies, and in that sense must become a metaphysician before he can work as a theologian.

In considering pragmatism (p. 189) or " philosophies of personal life " (p. 207), one cannot help comparing the differences in the theology that would result if these were accepted or rejected. It is not possible for a theologian to avoid a definite position in such choices, if he wishes to adopt his procedures openly and clearly. Pragmatism has declined in influence, and although the " philosophies of personal life " (as expounded, for example, by Martin Buber, Miguel de Unamuno, and Nicolas Berdyaev) still have wide popular appeal, they do not have much theological influence. In realizing this, the theologian may face the task of launching a philosophical revival (a task that can be accomplished), or he may formulate for his own purposes a supporting technical base that would be adequate for adapting popular insights to systematic theology. Thus, both the theology and its method are clarified and brought into sharper focus by the options that philosophy forces them to face.

The descriptive approach to theology which follows Husserl and phenomenology seems very much in vogue today in both Catholic and Protestant circles. Because of this, it is more important than ever for the theologian to inquire into the basic assumptions of this view and into its theological adequacy. The difficulty in making such an inquiry, as Macquarrie points out, is that this descriptive approach claims to be without presuppositions (p. 223). In one sense the claim is valid, because phenomenology attempts to pay primary attention to the given data. In another sense, however, its claim is not valid, because the whole mode of its philosophy requires a great deal more analysis, not only of its aims but of the basic assumptions involved in its very approach. For instance, can any given data ever interpret itself? Or is theology as interested in the phenomena before us as it is in its origins and directions? These questions might be ruled out by a descriptive approach, unless the theologian uses his method with a critical philosophical temper and first understands what that approach allows and does not allow.

Idealism once provided a very fruitful theological base when it combined, as it did for Hegel, both philosophy and theology. Idealism not only allowed for metaphysics, it was itself an elaborate metaphysics. With the violent reaction to idealism that has come about, theology, unless it can promote an idealist revival, must find an alternate base or else be swept away — at least for the moment.

For one who would seek a new philosophical basis for a contemporary theology it is perhaps the realist movement in

America and England that offers the greatest, although as yet unfulfilled, possibilities. Macquarrie points out that as this movement has developed it has in fact tended toward materialism and naturalism, which in themselves are not too congenial to theology (pp. 238–239). Realism has not always developed a metaphysics, beginning as it did as a theory of knowledge. Yet there is no reason why it cannot do so, and in fact a realist metaphysics might be a very powerful theological base particularly for those who cannot accept idealism's mind-centeredness.

Let us pause for a moment here and point out one example of the kind of theological advantage that a realist metaphysics can offer. In this view, mind ceases to be the center of things and the world exists independently of our knowing it. If objects exist independently from the mind's knowing process, and if it is at least possible for the mind to grasp an object, to know it as it is essentially unaffected and unaltered by the mind's mode of grasp, then God can exist as an independent object, whatever the mind's mode or limitations may be. Therefore, limitations on the mind's grasp and range are no longer in themselves an argument either for or against God's existence or for his nature in some particular form.

If realism as a theory takes an empirical turn, then it can often become theologically hostile, since God is seldom if ever an empirical object. If realism is not so limited in its scope, then God as an object of consideration can become one more independently existing object whose nature and ground for existence can be investigated. Realism opens the possibility for God's nature to contain qualities that are different in kind from mind and yet still basic to his nature. Idealism by definition prejudices us toward God, it is true, but still it is toward a mind-like God.

Recent scientific theory has not proved to be a very firm base for theological extension, but, if science is now neutral, then it is no longer as hostile as it often was in earlier times in its connection with materialism or naturalism. Whenever scientific theory seems to demand a certain kind of metaphysics, it poses real problems for theology. But when the physical sciences admit at least the possibility of a variety of theoretical bases and metaphysics, then the sciences neither encourage theology nor prevent it. Some liberal theologians have been antimetaphysical, which would be somewhat ironical if science has actually moved to a trust in reason and an open attitude that can tolerate theology of a metaphysical kind. This openness does not specify a certain kind of metaphysics, and the realists have in fact differed about the exact metaphysics that they feel inclined to accept. If the mind does not impose one metaphysics upon us, however, then realism should be compatible with a variety of developments. This may be the most advantageous situation for theology after all.

As realism developed toward the analysis of language, it reopened the possibility of considering theological statements, certainly an advantage over an earlier positivism that ruled them out. As Macquarrie says, however, for all the helpful clarity analysis provides for understanding the perhaps special status of religious statements, it does not appear to be a very congenial base for theological construction (p. 316). This is not so important in an age when powerful theologies have been formed that require only analysis for their understanding; but when an age is really most in need of new theological construction, then language analysis and empiricism of any radical sort do not appear to offer a very fruitful source.

Lack of congenial philosophical support may explain something about the development of powerful theological movements that exclude philosophy and deny that they have any dependence upon it. These "theologies of the Word" depend heavily on revelation. Finding out whether or not they are as free of philosophy as they suppose is not so important as finding out whether or not similar theological constructions that use a philosophical base also exist so that comparisons can be made. It is hard to determine whether a theology

is independent of philosophy unless it can be compared with
one that does not claim to be so free. Then the relative merits
of each can be appraised.

By contrast, existentialism has clearly sparked a theological
revival of its own, so that in some basic sense its theological
usefulness as a philosophy is beyond question. Its antirationalistic tendencies stand in interesting contrast to empiricism and language analysis, but unlike realism it does not
tend to inspire metaphysical construction. When existentialism as a way of approaching philosophy is brought together
with phenomenology, metaphysics of a certain type results
(e.g., the works of Sartre and Heidegger), but it is not realism.
This metaphysics, although clearly helpful to theology, also
suggests a problem: Can it move forward to develop a doctrine of God, or does its basis inhibit such an extension? It is
interesting that realist metaphysics (e.g., the works of Hartshorne and Whitehead) seems to lead quite naturally to a
doctrine of God, even if in some cases it leads to a limited
God.

Most of the questionable features of existentialism (e.g.,
subjectivism and irrationalism) can be kept under control by
the care of its followers, although it must be admitted that
existentialism by its very nature leads to extravagant statement. Yet, as Macquarrie says, one facet of existentialism that
cannot be altered without destroying its uniqueness is that
it makes our own human existence the locus for all philoso-
phizing (p. 370). Religion is obviously a phenomenon of
human existence, so that existentialism may be expected to
be most profound and insightful in interpreting this area of
human experience.

The usefulness of existentialism for theology depends on
the kind of theology that is wanted. If a theological framework is to be based on the nature of the mode of human existence and the interpretation of the experience that such a
context can provide, then existentialism's value has already

been proved. However, if theology's aim is toward a doctrine of the nature of God in some traditional sense, then the theology so far produced under existential influence seems to show that such an aim is difficult to achieve by means of existentialism.[8] Tillich perceived this difficulty, and he blends a mystical doctrine of God with his own existentialist interpretation of the human situation. The question then is whether these two different elements can be blended together or whether one element will tend to be rejected. In the case of Tillich it is probably God who will lose out, since existentialism is the dominant theme for Tillich.

In its analysis of human existence, existentialism (with or without phenomenology) can lead up to the idea of God, but it does not develop a metaphysical doctrine of God's nature to go along with the idea. A man of a religious disposition is not prevented from affirming God in this context (even Tillich's mystical God if one is inclined toward mysticism). The difficulty is that the philosophical approach does not itself provide the basis for achieving clarity on the nature of God. If evidence of God's nature was as obvious as the evidence of human existence, there might not be such a problem for theology. However, since we have no agreement about the nature of God to begin with, we seem to need, for theological purposes, a new philosophical base that can lead to the development of a clear concept of God. This concept should be available without having to add God to it from a different source, because such additions may or may not be accepted by those who follow existential analysis.

Macquarrie concludes by seeing a teeming diversity but no common view emerging (p. 371). This does not give the contemporary theologian much specific guidance, but the freedom to select options is perhaps in itself the most encouraging and important fact in the present theological situation. The novice in theology has sometimes felt either that he must reject philosophy in developing a theology or that he must work from one dominant philosophical source, perhaps in some revised form.

It is clear that both theology and philosophy have many meanings and that no one of them can be established to the permanent exclusion of all others. The theologian is free to appraise not only the advantages and the disadvantages of nonphilosophical theology but also the assets and the liabilities for theological purposes of each philosophical view without feeling that his existence at some time and place in itself limits him to a single choice. An examination of our age indicates that, in spite of the clamor of any one view at any one moment, an almost classical range and variety of philosophical sources are available for our approval.

The philosophical health of our day lies in its emancipation from the idea that any single view of philosophy or theology is required or is superior in every respect to all other views. This situation does not in itself produce vital new theologies, but at least there is a wide variety of choices available to us. What more can a theologian ask for as he assesses his situation in relation to philosophy in general and to some particular philosophical view?

Macquarrie, in developing his own line of thought from among the available alternatives, tends toward specific interpretations that are challengeable by anyone who does not share his assumptions (pp. 372–375). Further, Macquarrie quotes Bultmann to the effect that the question of God and the question of self are identical, which is perhaps the greatest single issue today and not one to be considered lightly (p. 376). The question is, What source can really produce a new doctrine of God for a theologian in our time?

This chapter has not aimed at being anything like a comprehensive survey of all the philosophical views available. Macquarrie's book has done that in a manner which is quite sufficient. Our aim has been to try to develop a philosophical base for theology and to suggest specifically what such a base could and should be like in the light of the situation. Thus, this brief analysis of the philosophical sources, together with a few critical indications, is merely prolegomena and raw material for later construction. Although it is too soon to make any final summations, two factors do emerge. (1) Theology's most obvious task today seems to be to develop a detailed doctrine of God, particularly one that is philosophically based. When we examine the current state of philosophy, it is easy to see why many philosophical views either restrict or inhibit such a task. Perhaps the first question that a theologian must ask today is whether he takes the development of a doctrine of God to be his central task; then he must ask which philosophical base will allow this development, to what degree, and with what obstacles or with what positive help.

A second factor needs to be pointed out by way of summary. (2) Philosophical innovators usually either have been ahead of their time or else have reached back to draw inspiration from some neglected theory of an earlier time. Although it does not aim to be a historical account, even Macquarrie's analysis of the present scene might leave the impression that theology can select only from among the views that are already clearly defined and established at present, which is not really the case. Of the views that Macquarrie presents, almost all have their roots in the nineteenth century or at least very early in the twentieth.

As noted in the last chapter, Protestant theology seems presently to be in a period of calm, and perhaps philosophy is too. In philosophy, most of the creative figures alive today are quite elderly. In addition to understanding twentieth-century thought as it has developed to date, our problem as far as theology is concerned is to try to outline a *future* philosophical base, even if it is one that is not presently dominating attention or even if it is not very vital at the moment. Theologically, the task may be one of philosophical revival or innovation rather than of contemporary acceptance. Here, of course, we are aided by the present situation in which, as a matter of fact, almost no philosophical view is completely absent. Philosophy by itself does not restrict our freedom of choice, and in that sense the situation today allows every approach for our use in the future.

IV *What do we need for a theology?*

BEFORE WE CAN GO any farther toward constructing a philosophical basis for theology, we have to establish what theology's needs are. We now know that our time alone does not dictate any one form of philosophy or theology. Thus, we are free to shape our theological goals with an eye to the current needs and situation, but we are not limited by them. We know that suggestions for the future may not in any direct sense come from the present day, although some characteristic fact or need either of the present or of the past may indicate a new mode.

When we determine what these special theological needs are as we see them, leaving others free to pursue their different needs, we can construct a philosophical basis for theology out of the elements of philosophy present in any age as well as in our own. Since we are not restricted to any one line of development, we are at liberty to pick our philosophy to fit our theological aims, but first we must establish what these aims are.

We might suspect at the end of an antimetaphysical era that theology has at times been the victim of metaphysics, and this often seems to have been the case. Philosophy can be nonmetaphysical (but only to a degree), and it can be limited when it confines itself temporarily to specific issues without regard to wider context. On the other hand, theology by its nature must have the kind of fundamental perspective that metaphysics has. Whenever it fails to develop a metaphysical outlook, theology tends to assume a certain philosophical attitude, such as Bultmann with his " modern man " or Tillich with existentialism. A philosophical basis must be argued for and not assumed, but this requires a metaphysically sensitive age. Such an age is engaged in questioning its basic definitions and assumptions, not just in stating them flatly and working out the theological implications. Ours seems to be a time when men are driven to theological conclusions, including atheism, by their metaphysical assumptions when instead they should use critical analysis of these assumptions as an aid to continuous theological development.

We need, then, *a metaphysically sensitive theology*. There are other forms for theology, but a revival of this metaphysical form might resolve some current confusion. We should be the masters of our basic framework and not its victims. Although not every option is open, there is more than one choice, and so we need metaphysical sensitivity in order to appraise with skill the theological consequences of the framework that is selected. This issue of metaphysics leads to the basic question of what role philosophy in general is to play in any theology. The problem is not a simple matter of defining our theological goals independently and then selecting a philosophical form in order to develop them. In the initial statement of any system of theology the role of philosophy must be indicated, and that cannot be done without raising the question of what philosophy is.

Since I have tried to state the basic nature of philosophy elsewhere I will not deal here with the fundamental question of what philosophy is.

It must be remembered, however, that no theology that reflects on its procedures can begin without working out its own view of what philosophy is. The method of this formulation will determine the role that philosophy can play in theology, for the nature of philosophy cannot be assumed but must be worked out. If philosophy was one single system and if it was given to us in one form, this investigation might not be necessary. Since philosophies are many and varied, each theologian must first become a philosopher in working out his own definition. It is most important to see the exact blend and combination of philosophy in the life of theology, which is something that can be determined only as the definition of philosophy is developed. This does not mean that the two fields of philosophy and theology cannot have some independence from one another, but it does mean that their definitions should correlate, i.e., they should be worked out in mutual dependence.

Theology is not helpless where philosophy is concerned. First of all, the theologian himself can work out his own view of philosophy, since no single view is dictated to him. Furthermore, theology contains elements other than philosophy, which also determine possible blends and combinations of views. Since theology has at least as many forms as philosophy does, our question is this, Which norm is to be accepted as final? Theology would seem to be defined by the ingredients that make it up, but what are these elements? (1) Philosophy, as it is worked out, is one element. (2) The second element from which theology usually draws its materials is that of a particular religious tradition, except when it is a pure philosophical extension from the metaphysical consideration of a first principle. (3) More specifically, this tradition usually involves the canon of a sacred literature. (4) Almost the most important element contributing to any one theology is the variety of previous theologies developed from these sources. These past theories are not determining elements in a contemporary theology, but they certainly do orient it and serve as a testing ground that can illustrate the consequences of assuming certain doctrines.

Other elements, depending on the particular type of theology proposed, are (5) the religious life of the individual and (6) the ritual practice and tradition of the religious community. Although they ought not to determine a theology, the perplexing issues of the day will give theology an orientation revolving around them (7). In any era certain problems (e.g., the nature of freedom) are more urgently in need of solution than others. The acceptance of certain questions as deserving top priority will tend to cause theology to arrange other questions around these issues. A theology may accept one of these elements (or portions of each of them) as definitive and this will give that theology its special nature. Previously developed formulas and definitions may be taken as a standard (8), but, even when they are, they do not carry their own interpretation with them but rather, since they are expressed in words, they need reworking in every age. In fact, no one of these eight elements has a single fixed definition, and each is often filled with multiple meanings (e.g., sacred literature). Without philosophy's refining power a comprehensible theology could not emerge.

Whatever else may be " given by God," theologies are not. Theology is always a composite made by us, whether made up of precisely the eight elements outlined above (which include philosophy) or drawn from some slightly different set of materials. The point is that theology is not given to us. As a compilation of words, it has no more permanence than words themselves have. Philosophy's crucial task is to determine the way in which these eight elements should come together to form a theology.

What do we need for theology? The first thing we need is *a rule defining and guiding the way in which its various elements come together.* Theology as a mixture of elements is not as pure or as basic a discipline as philosophy. Theology's form can never be taken for granted but must always be developed as an artificial construct, and as such it needs more philosophy than philosophy does itself. The role that philosophy plays in theology will be dictated by the way in which the theology is conceived, but philosophy always enters into any definition of theology from the very start.

" Revelation " is a complex subject that needs an extensive and separate treatment, but it should be briefly mentioned here. In developing a philosophical base for theology, one must remember that the meaning of revelation itself is not given, and that revelation, since it requires interpretation, is more a product of a theological view than it is a determining basis of that view. Thus, philosophy must enter theology before revelation can be defined since no single meaning for revelation is agreed upon. The religious community may accept revelation not philosophically defined, but theology cannot.

Revelation could be accepted as a single normative theological source only if its meaning were not in dispute; then theology might dispense with philosophy. As it is, however, any interpretation of the meaning of revelation is a task of philosophical definition. No matter what specific meaning is later given to revelation, which might then determine a theological doctrine, philosophy had to be available first in order to work out the meaning of revelation and to defend that definition and the peculiar role assigned to revelation in theology.

If revelation influences theology despite its philosophical limitations, it may produce a certain kind of theology, but it can never be sufficient in itself to supply all the needs of theological construction. There is more to the theological view than the proposed data of revelation, which must be philosophically refined in any case, in order to be definitionally sharp enough to be of any help to theology. Were theology placed in some medium other than words, this flexibility might not be true.

Theology is flexible because its definitions are not sharp, precise, and technical enough to serve as norms unless they are systematically structured by some particular philosophical terminology. The materials available in theology are even more vast and varied than they are for philosophy, so they can assume no clear form unless the technical intelligence of men refines and structures them into various views. Once these theological views are structured they can provide a clear focus and yield answers to our religious questions, but this focus is not provided by the raw material of theology when it is philosophically unaided.

It would seem, therefore, that whatever other forms theology might assume, one central form must always be developed by philosophical means. This being the case, what happens to theology if we lack the philosophical power to develop a new idea of philosophy itself in our own day? Or more specifically, what happens when the new ideas in philosophy are not particularly congenial to theology, or when those which might be congenial are metaphysically lacking? Then theology must flounder, since its own materials are too varied and too disparate to fuse together without a philosophical catalyst.

Theology rightfully fears philosophy as a competitor for the allegiance of men and sometimes even as a negative opponent that can deny theology the right to live. It is equally true that theology should fear the lack of a vigorous philosophy; theology needs a congenial and particularly a metaphysical philosophy. Without this the very variety of theology's materials might overwhelm it and drive it along without allowing it a control over its direction and conclusions. If theology's sources were not so varied or so disparate in their raw form, theology might not be so philosophically dependent.

Specifically we need to ask: What can make God real for thought today? He may or may not be real for any individual's religious life or for a particular tradition, but it seems evident that, however real, this personal God is not the same as having a concept of God for systematic thought, and an abstract concept of God is perhaps what theology is least clear about today. Ironically, the nonphilosophical materials of theology can be very useful until they are faced with working out a systematic analysis of the divine nature; when it comes to abstractions these materials are so scanty or enigmatic that only philosophy and metaphysics can produce a systematic analysis with the needed clarity. Whenever this is not done, then the nature of God fades for thought. If it is not conscious of the philosophical and theological alternatives available where God is concerned, theology can lose control of its directions (e.g., in humanism) or even deny God as theologically useful.

It seems obvious that the first thing we need for theology is a philosophy capable of developing a concept of God and of sustaining it for critical appraisal and for application to the development of specific theological views. The first problem any theology must deal with systematically is the nature of God. In reviewing and appraising its philosophical options, theology must first investigate how each of the various available forms of philosophy treats God and what each will and will not allow.

We cannot say simply that some philosophical forms allow God and others do not. Instead, for each one the approach to God will vary greatly. Although partly determined by the order of priority which is given to philosophical questions, it depends primarily on how directly this approach touches the questions of God's nature and what kind of God is implicit in each theory. It would be easy if theology had its concept of God given to it already systematically defined. Whatever raw materials theology may begin with, its mode and the extent of its development of the concept of God depend still on the philosophy adopted.

We need a clear, full, concept of God in a theology, but more than one philosophy can accomplish this, each in varying ways and degrees. We will take up later the question of what kind of philosophy it should be and what modes are adequate for this task from philosophy's side. At present, we must get a clearer picture of theology's needs, particularly against the background of its current forms and specifically with reference to the question of a concept of God.

We have denied any simple evolutionary pattern in theological theory. If in some sense all options are now open to us, it must be that in any age some alternatives are more needed than others, perhaps in order to offset an unhealthy balance of theological views. At no time can all possible theological forms be equally healthy and influential, so that the needs of theology tend to become evident from an examination of the weaknesses of the current scene.

First of all, we need to know the composition and purpose of the elements of theology, since only by understanding these can any analysis of theology's most pressing needs be made. Basically, the elements of theology are very much like philosophy's, but as indicated in the outline above, theology is far less simple in its data than philosophy. Understanding theology's complex nature is the first requirement of theology, but that kind of analysis is the business of philosophy. With the basic understanding of the stuff of theology, we can proceed to examine the current theological trends. From their weaknesses, we can form a clearer picture of which presently undeveloped forms of theology should be stressed for healthy balance and variety.

Now we can shift to consider the proposal for an " American theology " by asking: What are the various current trends in theology, and what can we learn from these about our future theological needs? If we can answer these questions, then we can examine our philosophical options to see how these satisfy our theological needs. Variety of opinion — heterodoxy — was the first characteristic quality we noted in the American theological situation. If an indigenous new theology is to be built, then a philosophical theory is required that permits many different doctrines — and not all do. Some philosophies are so developed and self-sufficient that no other viewpoint is allowed. Such an outlook does not lead to the development of a theology that would embrace the distinctive features of the American scene, because our primary distinction and the first need of our pluralistic society is for a philosophy that does not exclude variety of opinion and pluralism by its basic assumptions.

Radical theology is in some sense an American phenomenon, although other forms originating in Europe have adopted philosophical principles which lead both to the exclusion of God and to many unorthodox beliefs. In the subtlety of their interpretation, however, continental forms of theology often can keep up the appearance of tradition. But in the blunt honesty of the American manner, the radical theologians openly state that these premises, which ultimately end in an exclusion of God, lead away from tradition. This tells us two things about our needs in theology: (1) An American theology should be characterized by its use of a simple and direct approach, avoiding the circumlocutions which are able to hedge the conclusions that follow from its premises. It should be characterized by its use of simple and direct statement, avoiding the mystical vagueness of the continental profundity of style. It can be metaphysically proficient and technically abstract — as proficient and abstract as American scientists are in their fields — but American theology should depend on a straightforward simplicity of language. (2) An American theology needs the ability to develop a doctrine of God, since that is the doctrine most underdeveloped on the current theological scene. Radical theology by its excesses is a good indication of what is needed in American theology.

Tillich, on the other hand, is both philosophical and mystical in his theology, and this approach seems to have a wide reception in America. We need his open acceptance of a philosophical framework, so that the fruitfulness of his theology may be appraised; however, his view of philosophy seems too exclusive. Tillich's thought seems to limit the possibility of other definitions of philosophy and theology. We need a theology that allows for more than one mode of philosophy and theology and also for a nonmystical view of God — not that mysticism is in any way unacceptable, but our current need is for a direct doctrine of God to balance the mystical approach, which is not indigenously American.

As we noted in the discussion of Tillich, we need a major theologian, or perhaps several, to follow the earlier generation. Does the lack of major new theologians perhaps indicate that our basic assumptions are not sound and that we need a new starting point? Any such starting point should rediscover Niebuhr's ethical and social concern, but we can see that this also needs to be embedded in a larger systematic structure. Bonhoeffer can give us a lead here too. We require secular involvement, but we also need this to be within the context of a more complete and technical theology.

Any theology that is both American and Protestant cannot fail to include an intense social concern and interest in the welfare of others. Now the test is to see whether America can come of age intellectually in theology (as it must in other areas too), not only to preserve both its native practical drive and its social concern, but at the same time to ground these in a philosophical context, which has carefully developed metaphysical premises. America has sometimes been antimetaphysical, but this is a luxury of youth that now must be surrendered for maturity.

America was never much impressed with the church as an institution, and in fact we framed our Constitution to play down its power. America is not given to establishing religious groups so rigid and incompatible that they are unable to communicate. In this sense Barth's *Church Dogmatics* is not congenial to the American tradition. Whatever contribution it might make, we need a theology which is not rigid in its basic approach and which is open to all for appraisal without prior commitment. It would seem to follow that America's natural mode is philosophical theology. Along with this approach we could develop a lay theology, one that would not be the product of our professionals, the clergy, whom we have never recognized as our superiors. Our theology may come from the church, but it should never be exclusively for the clergy or for those already admitted to " the club " by their prior acceptance of a given perspective.

The case of Bultmann illustrates the need for clear philosophical assumptions that do not rule out traditional beliefs at the outset or force a compromise with the New Testament message. Americans cannot long accept this indecision, as the radical theologians testify. Biblical theology demonstrates both theology's great need and its most fruitful tendency. A clear understanding of what the Biblical documents say is absolutely crucial in clearing the theological stage for a new performance. If the Biblical theological movement could be separated from its connection with one special philosophical outlook, and opened to an association with many philosophical forms, then it might spark a theology, but only if these philosophies are conducive to a full expression of the essential New Testament proclamation.

At least one thing Biblical theology tells us clearly is that it alone cannot give an adequate theory of the nature of God. Therefore Biblical theology, almost more than any other form, requires the addition of philosophical thought in order to include God. On the other hand, fundamentalism, or conservative theology, is strong in its Biblical orientation, but herein lies its danger. Its initial anti-intellectualism makes it suspicious of philosophy. Fundamentalism, like Biblical theology, is one of the forms of theology that most needs philosophy if it is to have a clear concept of God. A knowledge of the writing of historical figures also demonstrates this need, for it is evident that each author has relied upon some philosophical framework of his own day to write his theology and to describe God's nature.

We must realize that the gospel message cannot be conveyed in a pure form, unmodified by past or present modes of thought. In recognizing this lack of purity, we can be consciously philosophical, knowing that even Biblical statements are obscured by layer upon layer of different interpretations

and perspectives. Still, some men have put an end to this uncertainty by controlling their selection of philosophical
sources so they can use these sources as guides to express whatever they want to say with authority and clarity.

Theology needs to learn it is not forced into any particular
mold by philosophy or by its times. To learn this, theology
must have a variety of options, a heterodoxy, to choose from,
so that a theology's form is not determined simply by its lack
of choice. Americans can call on their vast heritage of past
sources and through these escape the provincialism of the
present moment. Here America's openness to every trend
should reflect itself in the theology it constructs. Such a theology should be without an antimetaphysical tone and should
be congenial to systematic effort.

If we are in a lull after a storm of theological activity, and
if the radical theologians are only discovering too late what
was contained in their philosophical assumptions, then theology needs a new direction. This direction should make
possible a missionary outreach. The theology itself does not
need to be evangelical, but its form should allow a powerful
preaching of the gospel in fresh terms. It must not be intramural or meaningful only to the initiated. It must reach out,
but not by becoming secular, for then it has nothing unique
to report. Here the doctrine of God is crucial. If we are able
to develop an adequate contemporary concept of God, then
this doctrine can once again explain God's actions to the unbelievers, which is theology's first task.

We need a theology today that does not exclude all forms
other than its own, but which allows theology's full variety to
be possible. Biblical, dogmatic, sociological, ethical, psychological historical, and comparative religion are all possible
modes of developing theology, although one need not value
them all equally or become insensitive to the limitations of
each perspective. It is not, then, a question of there being
" one theology." There are many, and any theology must account for this fact internally. This does not mean, however,

that we are able to accept them all.

Given the current possibilities in theology, we must ask: What is presently lacking? Is there a crucial absence or weakness, and how can a strong theological mode be provided for or reestablished? Today in American Protestant circles, the answer to these questions seems to be that a metaphysics of the divine nature is a theological necessity, but that this form of theology is committed to a prior philosophical inquiry in order to establish itself.

When we consider the relation of philosophy to our current theological needs, it is clear that some theologies require less philosophy than others. If it is a metaphysics of the divine nature that we lack and want, this would perhaps be the most philosophically dependent form of theology. Can philosophy today support this crucial theological need? Actually, philosophy could always support a metaphysical theology, and it can do so today. With the availability of classical sources and the knowledge that our time will not impose a particular metaphysics on us, we have learned that theology is not bound to any single philosophy as a source, no matter how domineering it may appear at the moment. Although it is just as dangerous for philosophy to bind itself to one fashion as it is for theology to do this, theology must of necessity be more wary of current fashions. By its nature, theology must gather its sources from a full range of traditional questions and answers.

In answering the question raised by this chapter, we have tried to uncover theology's current needs, and specifically we have tried to see how these needs can be met by philosophy. Next we will consider what kind of philosophy we can provide to accomplish this. Philosophy may not be equally important for all kinds of theology, but, for the theological needs described in this chapter, a congenial and a helpful philosophical base is almost crucial. Our current theological crisis would really seem to be a philosophical crisis, since the kind of theology that is needed — and which is not presently available — requires the support of a philosophy with certain special metaphysical features. The state of Protestant theology today is so precarious that there should be an immediate and extensive philosophical search for the needed metaphysics. At any rate, without this basic metaphysical philosophy, Protestant theology does not seem able to keep its God alive.

V *What kind of philosophy can we provide?*

THE FIRST CHAPTER tried to outline briefly what kind of philosophy might be needed; the next chapters surveyed the present theological and philosophical situations; the fourth chapter discussed our theological needs today. At this point, the time has come to be a little more specific about just what philosophy can and cannot provide as a basis for a contemporary Protestant theology. It must be clear that there are many bases of philosophy just as there are many sources of theology. It should not be necessary to examine each philosophical basis. What we want to do at this point is to see whether, in the light of our peculiar theological needs and weaknesses, a philosophical basis can be formed to provide an answer to the special needs of the day.

What will the particular philosophical basis which we propose here be like? If we can list its attributes, it may be easier to determine if in fact it is possible to produce such a philosophy. (1) Its first characteristic, one which has been mentioned before, is that it should be nondogmatic about its exclusiveness but characterized instead by an openness to alternatives and reformulations. (2) Its second attribute is that it must be free, using " freedom " as a guiding concept, not just as a by-product of other principles. Unpredictable contingency must be allowed for, and a lack of certainty and necessity admitted. (3) A third attribute of a basic philosophy for these purposes is that it should show a sensitivity to the subtle shifts of meaning and to the necessity for technical terms. It must recognize that it is difficult to fix meaning with such precision that no further changes in interpretation are possible.

(4) For theological purposes, almost the most important attribute of a philosophical base must be that it is not exclusively empirical but open to speculative extension and to theoretical formulation. (5) This philosophy should make possible a metaphysical inquiry into first principles and a construction of a general theory of Being although this may be accomplished in any one of several ways.[4] (6) It might do this by using the new psychology pioneered by existentialism, in which metaphysical concepts can be related to and grounded in a different meaning of experience, rather than being limited to the empirical observation of sense data.[5] Such a philosophical basis cannot " prove " theological doctrine or confirm religious belief. (7) But at least it should be capable of formulating doctrine without making any given traditional belief impossible simply by its use of some form of philosophy. However, this use of philosophy requires further investigation to see whether it can express theological questions without necessarily distorting or restricting traditional beliefs, if reestablishing such belief is theology's goal.

(8) This philosophy, if it aims to be a basic support of theology, should not be primarily *self*-oriented, as so much recent philosophy and even metaphysics has been. Intense, even morbid, interest in the self is perhaps religion's worst tendency, so that any philosophical form that encourages preoccupation with self seems to underscore (rather than to play down) a tendency that is capable of distorting both theological doctrine and Christianity's message. A philosophical basis in which the self occupies the whole center of attention makes it hard for theology to resist egotism and self-centeredness. However valuable the self may be as a center for cer-

tain philosophical developments, a shift from this emphasis seems required today.

(9) Philosophy should also be independent of the prevailing interests and attitudes of the day. By its nature it is not supposed to be the victim of current ideas. It should not be driven by any passing fashions, but instead should stand apart from them and be their critic. This is really the most valuable contribution of philosophy to theology, and here is where a philosophical base is most needed. Theology, partly because of its connection to religion and partly because of the nature of the problems with which it deals, is often vulnerable to the immediate fashions of thought and frequently is more involved in dealing with present problems. Philosophy, if it fulfills its Socratic ideal, can release theology from this dangerous tendency to be too contemporary and unduly influenced by the concerns and thoughts of the hour. In one sense, theology is more oriented toward a timeless perspective on problems than is philosophy, but in another sense theology is less free from the tyranny which the present moment can exercise over thought. Philosophy must help in its emancipation.

(10) Another aspect to be noted about this needed philosophical base is that it should not have a historically determined view. This view, which represents only one, not very obvious, philosophical theory regards our thought forms as the products of our present cultural setting and its historical past. Even when such a theory sees Christianity or some religious spirit as a part of the historical process, this historical determination of thought need not be accepted if it seems incompatible with theology's aims. If it accepts this view uncritically, theology has no independence from the historical situation and cannot build on other philosophical grounds. Philosophy can free theology from historically determined thought, but only if theology selects for itself a mode of philosophy that is not historically dominated. In order to free theology, philosophy must have the ability to deal with non-

temporal thought as well as to explore the modes of Being that are subject to time.

We have listed here some of the fundamental philosophical characteristics that we need to know about in order to build a philosophical base; let us now turn back for a moment to see what can or cannot be contributed by the philosophical sources outlined in Chapter III. As has been suggested already, a new terminology might come from existentialism, and also perhaps the formation of a new basis for metaphysics. Although this cannot be undertaken without some revision of existentialism's original antimetaphysical bent, it is possible that existentialism might have unintentionally provided a basis for such a formation.[6] Without an explicit extension in the direction of metaphysics, however, existentialism may remain limited by an overconcentration on the self. If it remains so limited, existentialism is not necessarily a good basis for a theological discussion of God's nature.

Phenomenology, which often is joined to an existential mode of thought, seems subject to the same qualifications, i.e., a methodological prejudice against speaking directly about God and a tendency toward concentration on the self and on only the temporal modes of Being. In these respects, it also is limited in its theological application. Process philosophy, on the other hand, promises a new view of God, and its basis in realistic thought enables it to escape a too exclusive concentration on self-analysis. The issues here are the reconciliation of the process philosopher's view of God with the traditional view of divine attributes.[7] Even more important for a Christian theology, God must be capable of performing the kinds of actions which the Christians claim have come from him (e.g., salvation). We must also ask if this form of philosophy is inevitably connected to some one theory of evolution. A new view of time is involved, it is true, but does this result in a classically omnipotent God or a limited God, and are the powers of a limited God sufficient for all that we require for a theology?

Analytic thought may give us a fresh understanding of the status of our theories and of the verbal tools with which we work, but except as it is accidentally connected, it is not a substantive metaphysics nor can it yield a theory of God on its own basis. As a philosophy this is not unacceptable, depending on one's objectives; it is just that analytic thought is not very helpful theologically beyond a certain point.

Kant's " moral law " might once have been a fair approach to God, but not all ethical theory is theologically useful. In fact, it may currently be up to theology to try to revive an interest in a broad spectrum of ethical problems and action, which would indicate that ethical theory cannot presently be looked to for much help in forming a theological base. In our era, it may be the other way around; in an age that has challenged its values, ethical norms cannot be assumed as basic but must be drawn from another source.

Pragmatism has been out of fashion for some time, and yet it could form at least part of a theological base. It might have a valuable contribution to make, perhaps not in the detail of its early formulations but in its general orientation. Although pragmatism in the past often tended to be antispeculative, by nature it is tentative and open to other theories and to revision. Like existentialism, it was born in the era of Hegelian dominance. Could its fear of the dogmatic character of metaphysics be overcome (e.g., by building up a nondogmatic metaphysics), then it might be very helpful theologically. For instance, we learn from pragmatism, when it is coupled with speculative thought about God, to appraise the various theories, not only internally for their logical consistency, but also by asking which theories about God work. How does each concept of God "solve" the religious problems facing us?

Since the contemporary philosophical scene is not totally hostile to metaphysics and yet has not of itself produced a basis particularly congenial to metaphysics, something apparently still needs to be added. What is this missing element? Here again we come to the crucial balancing role that may be played by classical sources and theories. If we are freed from the idea that current theories must only reflect the trends of our own time, we are once again able to reach out to any classical theory when its qualities are needed for perspective or balance. This is not to suggest either a simple return to some single past view or a wholesale adoption of any system of traditional views, but instead the accumulation of classical theories as an anchor against undue contemporary influence and as a source from which to gain perspective on the present scene. Thus, *the appropriation of classical philosophical sources may be the crucial element needed in American theological development today.*

The availability of accumulated classical sources may be the catalyst we need in order to form a philosophical basis for contemporary Protestant theology. An ability to explore at will every established philosophical theory would give us a generous supply of elements, some of which may be missing on the contemporary scene. It is well known that contact with an earlier source may often suggest to a contemporary author some deficiency in his own time and may also lead to a beginning of new means of correction. If poorly handled, this exploration can be simply an indiscriminate eclecticism. At its optimum, it can be the invigorating process that is necessary for finding the essence of a new philosophical view.

Realism is a case in point. As this movement developed in America and in England, it was a reaction against the dominance of idealism. In its specific formulation, realism has certain features tied to contemporary problems, but as an epistemological theory its roots go back as far as Aristotle. As we read Aristotle, it becomes obvious that an alternative to idealism is possible, and then the particular form of realism's present application can be worked out. Realism as an epistemological view might have certain possibilities as a distinctively American philosophical base. In another general sense, as a nonromantic view of life, realism is also characteristic of an American attitude and might provide a base for a native theory of knowledge.

All these factors do not make up some new " American school " of philosophy. We have tried to show that the American philosophical scene is characteristically free from the attitude of " schools " and the necessity to argue philosophy in this form. Instead of a " school," we might have an assembly of elements, of basic principles that are available for our use and which are characterized by a variety of forms rather than some one form. American thought might be new and lack dependence on inherited forms, and yet at the same time it is free to accept philosophical suggestion from every ancient source, just as America itself has accepted its people from every land. The future of an American Protestant theology based on this spirit is a matter for more specific discussion in Chapter VII.

As far as the kind of philosophy that we need is concerned, there are still a few issues to be settled. We have canvassed the dominant philosophical trends mentioned in Chapter III, and our conclusion has to be that at present philosophy offers only a limited support to theology. The dominant philosophical trends today are not very conducive to the elaborations of systematic theology, which means that a suitable philosophical base is more difficult to develop than it would be under different circumstances. If we take the view, however, that we are not restricted to the present but can change it and add the whole store of past theories to it, then the situation for theology, while still difficult, is at least not desperate.

If we need a framework of the kind indicated by Chapter IV, our main question is whether there are now philosophical theories in existence powerful enough to generate such a framework. If such philosophies do not presently exist, our first theological task is the difficult job of philosophical reconstruction. Theology might rightly fear this preliminary diversion of its energies, especially if philosophy were to dictate theology's answers to its questions or even determine theology's conception of itself. In self-defense a theologian should first assess his needs, and then, becoming a philosopher himself, he should work within the available forms of theory to build the basis most suitable to his purposes. For a theologian to neglect this philosophical groundwork would actually be the most dangerous omission possible, because the form of theology itself could then be undermined by an intrusion of unselected philosophical elements, elements which had not been critically compared with their alternatives by a conscious process.

Theological needs, then, call for the kind of philosophy that is suitable to their own purposes. This philosophy is not easy to supply if philosophy is thought of only as a method of thought and not as a substantive doctrine also. Theology may think of philosophy strictly as a method, but, if we are right and if the theological view itself tends to become a metaphysical view of philosophy, then the substantive answers that philosophy gives to questions can in themselves form theological answers. Where philosophy is basically metaphysical, it takes as its primary task the delineation of the structures of all of Being. In this situation, the forming of a philosophical view shades almost imperceptibly into the consideration of specific theological questions. The major point to note here is that it makes a difference to theology whether philosophy is thought of as strictly methodological or whether philosophy is thought of as working out a basic doctrine of its own.

In either case the theologian must become his own philosopher in self-defense. If we are released from a dependence on our historical situation for our philosophical sources, then the theologian need not fear even a currently unfavorable climate. Philosophy has been congenial and conducive to theology in many previous eras, and these philosophies too are open to any theologian for his recovery and updating as each suits his need. If we have a philosophy that is characterized by freedom, flexibility, and contingency, one that is speculative by nature and not deterministic, then there is a philosophic atmosphere in which the theologian can work without fear of having his goals artificially restricted simply because of his philosophical context.

A reader who has thus far been patient might lose his patience at this point and demand, " Are we really free to have any philosophical view we want, as if we were choosing vegetables at the market? " For this essay, this question is perhaps the most crucial that might be asked, since it is true that our whole discussion has proceeded on an implicit assumption that we are that free, although certain limits will be outlined below. If this assumption is not true, if in any important sense our philosophy is either dictated to us or required to be of one kind, then this whole attempt to find a suitable philosophical basis for a contemporary theology would be beside the point. It would not be a route we are free to take, because the shaping of philosophy would be done for us in one way or another.

In considering the question of our freedom to form a philosophy for our own purposes, perhaps we are prejudiced even in our approach to this issue by having assumed too long that our philosophy is set for us rather than that we are able to compose one. Yet in order to explore this question farther, we need to try to set some limits on this freedom to form philosophical views, since freedom has real meaning only when its limits are determined. It is perfectly clear from the beginning that we are not free to adopt just any view we please. To see what options we do have, we must first rule out the alternatives not open to us; then we can try to establish the criteria by which the possible philosophical views might be ruled acceptable.

Of course, in one sense, a person is free to have any philosophical view he wants; it is impossible to legislate against an idea, even if a person's external habits may be regulated. Thus, the presence of some community of current belief would seem to be the first minimum requirement (1), but this must quickly be qualified so that it is not understood as a momentary popularity contest. Philosophy in its basic spirit should be immune to trends of fashion, but, sooner or later, each philosophical view must find some minds who can appropriate its doctrine and work within it, at least to some degree.

In order to assess this, any acceptable philosophical outlook must tie into the philosophical tradition at some point (2). This need not mean strict adherence to a philosophical " school," whether past or present, but it does mean that the problems taken up and the solutions provided must be able to establish a continuity with various traditions. The new formulations to questions and the use of new technical terms can be understood in comparison with the traditional material from which they evolved. Literal and faithful adherence to the previous material is not essential, since an advance often comes through understanding an ancient question or an old formulation in a new way. In that sense, any present view must be understood and appraised on its own, but still it should be comprehensible in relation to the established views from which it has departed. No theory of historical development or sequence needs to be assumed here, since any philosopher speaks more to the community of philosophers who preceded him than he does to his contemporaries.

Yet in another way, every revisionist philosopher speaks to the future too. If his motives are genuine and if he does not write wholly for present fame, then he reforms philosophy because he thinks it needs to have a new direction or a revival of a neglected question or forgotten interest. Here the philosopher in framing his new view must face the pragmatic test (3). Does the view work? Can others use it and think within its structure? Not that it must be immediately acclaimed or applied, but over the years it must find some acceptance and employment. If this acceptance is not found, it does not mean that the philosopher is wrong or that an individual cannot hold that philosophical view, but it does mean that the philosophy he has built is somehow lacking if it is not used fruitfully by others.

How can a philosophy make itself useful? If we consider this too narrowly, it may rule out too much. Although such a definition needs more detail, a philosophy is " useful " when an attentive mind can find that the solution to some problem is made possible, within the terms provided, in a way that could not be accomplished without that doctrine. This may be practical, as in ethics or politics, when a certain type of conduct is shown to be the proper response to an unclear situation. Or it may be theoretical, as when a dilemma of the mind is solved, or when some aspect of the general structure of Being is brought to light, or when some feature of God's nature is made plain in a way that could not be grasped without that theory.

We must now attempt to describe what goes into a philosophical view and how it is formed. In that sense, one basic criterion for the acceptability of any philosophical view is to test it in terms of the elements which we know all philosophical theory is made of and also to appraise its function in terms of such an analysis (4) . By using these elements a philosophy can be formed if it is found to have the effect on the minds of its readers which philosophy is understood to have. Given the elements of philosophy and the rules for their combination, any view that can meet these standards has at least a minimal acceptability.

This does not mean that every view propounded is as clear or as forceful in its results as every other. Some weak, almost irrelevant, nearly nonsensical views have been formed. Like the physical sciences, however, we do not want to restrict theoretical formations in philosophy by ruling out any view in advance, since we know that current plausibility is not a safe rule to apply. Philosophy is not without its tests, but unless some specific (probably empirical) view of philosophy is accepted as encompassing all of philosophy, philosophy never has the same solid experimental context that the natural sciences have. Its testing process takes a longer time as men's minds work over the theory propounded. Philosophy can be useful and practical, but in a more restricted sense than scientific theory.

A philosophical view which asserts that there is only one philosophical theory or one which claims that the philosophy we adopt is not freely selected but is determined for us (e.g., by social context or historical forces) must be admitted as possible philosophical views. Where theology is concerned, we must even admit the view that a theology may determine the philosophy with which it is associated. In an attitude of openness, these views must be admitted as possible philosophies, even though they involve us in internal contradiction, a problem which all good logics seem to have to face. For each of these views, in claiming exclusive truth for itself, would deny that it is simply one among a series of possible philosophies. Thus they deny the existence of a realm where many possible philosophical views are available despite our generous offer to admit each view as one among many.

Like any logic that generates a paradox, a way must first be found to deal with this before the details of a particular theory can be worked out more fully. In this case, the only way to deal with this internal contradiction is to point out to every student of philosophy that, before he can proceed, he must make a critical choice. If he elects the view that there is only one philosophy or that the philosophy he adopts is prescribed for him by whatever forces are outlined, then he rules out the idea that a range of philosophical views exists. This philosophy will then proceed in a quite separate direction and manner, perhaps by means of some historical analysis. On the other hand, if he elects the view that a variety of philosophies are possible, however wide or narrow this variety may be, he still leaves as admissible those philosophies which claim exclusive truth, although no longer in the form that they claim for themselves.

A somewhat more subtle problem is involved if a philosophy claims to be only a method, not substantive in doctrine but only methodological. British analytic thought stemming from Wittgenstein is probably a case in point. Since our interest is not in analyzing the claims of any single view but in questioning whether it can provide the basis that theology requires, we need only point out that analytic thought is merely one view of philosophy and clearly not the only possible one. Thus, it must be appraised for its possible metaphysical assumptions and assessed in relation to other possible views of philosophy. Although the issue of a philosophy that claims only to be a methodology is in some way special, basically such a point of view is still only one way of raising the question of the nature of philosophy and its possible modes. Such an important issue ought not to be taken for granted and can only be assessed by defining what the various alternatives to this view are.

At this point, the only real way to settle the question that this chapter raises would be actually to construct a particular philosophical view and then to test it for its theological versatility, just as Aquinas once tested Aristotle. Unfortunately, it is not the nature of philosophy to allow this to be done simply. It is important and it can be done, but only by working out carefully the general view of philosophy. However, a particular theory can only be stated by selecting one strain of philosophy and then working detailed material into that and moving on to deal with a series of problems. This is what happens to philosophy when it is appropriated theologically. Our task here is not to examine a particular philosophy or theology but rather to set out the various bases upon which philosophy might be most fruitfully used by theology.

As one example, let us take an issue that is crucial to theology and see what kind of philosophy is involved and whether it can be made available. Perhaps the primary question facing theology today is, Can we provide a philosophy that will allow us to speak directly about God? If we review Chapter III, it is interesting to see how few contemporary philosophies are able to answer this question affirmatively. Existentialism does not by nature do this, although I have suggested elsewhere [8] that a new metaphysics might be built on it that would allow what the existentialists themselves did not intend. Phenomenology by nature is directed toward exploring material that is unlikely in itself to reveal God as an object. Process philosophy can develop and has developed a new view of God, which seems to indicate that a realistic metaphysics may provide one answer to this question.

The next question to ask is, How adequate is that concept of God? British analytic thought would by nature seem uncongenial at this point. But if statements about God can be admitted for examination, then God is not excluded; the question then becomes one of the adequacy of analytic thought for constructing a new view. This is where the classical historical theories become crucial. In an era when the philosophical alternatives seem either to restrict or to be uncongenial to theological aims, then the revival, or at least the inspiration, of classical theories becomes an essential corrective. If philosophy were ever limited to its current options, it would cease to be philosophy, i.e., a critical appraisal of basic assumptions. To provide detachment from exclusive involvement in the present, classical theories must be kept as an ever-present alternative.

An ethical approach may or may not allow discussion about God. Since such discussion is in no way essential to an ethical question, ethics cannot be counted on to provide a basis upon which to discuss God. Idealism seems often to be involved with theories about the divine nature, but if it has temporarily exhausted its fruitfulness, other stimulation is needed. Philosophies of history may be either secular or religious and so deserve no special attention where God is the concern. Cultural and sociological theories will always reveal religion as a phenomenon, but it is questionable whether they can serve as a systematic basis for any new construction of the divine nature.

To see what kind of philosophy can be provided, and then to test each philosophy to see whether it can yield direct discussion about the possibility of God, is perhaps the central concern of theology. Although theology fears that philosophy may in some way dictate a particular view about the nature of God, such domination can be controlled if the philosophical form is picked cautiously. Of course, the terms and the general form will be shaped by the particular philosophical approach. As long as philosophy is not limited to one mode, the theologian can select according to his needs. If he picks wisely, he need have no fear of being coerced.

It is more often the case that theologians are dominated by the assumption that they are offered only one philosophical form to be either followed or rejected without alternative. It would seem that the perspective on philosophy most congenial to theology would be the one which would allow various possible alternatives and which would not be restricted to only one form in any day. With classical theories included, little is held back from theology's use. In such a situation theology should not fear dominance by some one tyrannical view of philosophy, but rather it should be concerned with its ability to handle philosophy and to mold the variety of alternatives that are open to it into one effective medium.

The answer to the question asked in the title of this chapter, What kind of philosophy can we provide? is that we can provide any kind of philosophy we need, within the limits of what philosophy is, has been, and can become, and what its elements can combine to form. That is a fairly broad answer, and it is hard to see how any theology could fail to find its requirements within this view. As an example of how this answer can be applied in some particular instance, take the issue regarding the status of " concepts." If a " concept " can provide a clear focus on the nature of God, within which the mind can orient itself to discuss the particulars of the divine nature, then that is a philosophical quality that is crucial to any theology. How we define such terms as " concept " is an important issue for fundamental theological decision. It might not be so vital if crucial terms were neutral or stable in their definition. Instead, definitions require constant effort on our part to sustain their meaning.

In one form or another, then, any theology should raise the question of the status of concepts (or universals or ideas) and ask what various answers lead to as far as their theological implications go. Were we forced to accept one outcome in this matter, the situation would be different. If we adopt a philosophy that itself allows for alternatives in philosophy, however, then we may pick and choose. But we should do so with care, with an eye to the criteria involved and to the consequences.

The possibility of metaphysics and the status given to it is another vital issue for theologians, in addition to the issues of God and concepts. If God were not used in theology as a first principle, then the question of metaphysics might not be so crucial. As it is, if metaphysics is not possible, or if it is severely restricted, or if it must take a special form, then this is of prime theological concern, since it will shape both what can be said about God and how it will be said. In *The Existentialist Prolegomena*, I suggested a new basis for metaphysics. The merits and demerits of this suggestion are not crucial, but a solution to the question of metaphysics is something that no theologian can avoid searching for. His work commits him to metaphysics, so that his solution to this problem will substantially affect his doctrine.

In a comparison of this chapter with the summaries in Chapters II and III, it should be obvious that theology has certain pressing needs today (e.g., for direct discussion of God) and that many of philosophy's present forms are not very conducive to fulfillment of these needs. Were we bound to one philosophical medium, we would have no escape and would simply have to do the best we could with prevailing views. But since we have established the case for some variety in philosophical view and for some flexibility in the selection of the various alternatives, the first effect of recognizing the incompatibilities on the philosophical-theological scene should be to spark a philosophical revolution. Perhaps we can also be inspired by the contrasts provided by the range of classical views that is open to us.

In Chapter IV we suggested theology's needs, so that in spelling out the form of philosophy required and in attempting to see whether it could be provided, we have anticipated that the answer will depend mainly on the special needs of a particular set of theological goals as they are outlined. We have suggested that these goals ought to include: a metaphysically oriented philosophy, a philosophy that can make discussion about God concrete, a philosophy that can speak to those who are not already committed to that view, and a philosophy that does not in its assumptions rule out the possibility of traditional Christian claims. These are fairly broad needs, and there perhaps have been times when theology's demands on philosophy were less. Today, unless these needs can be met, theology, will be severely restricted in what it can accomplish. If we have established that philosophy has some flexibility in its form, then our answer to this chapter's question can be that providing an appropriate philosophy is not an impossible task, and that in fact such a philosophy may be a reasonable alternative to the views that are dominant today.

If we severely restrict the range of possible philosophies, then theology is limited to what one view or its simple alternatives will allow. On the other hand, if we expand the range of acceptable philosophies to the widest number that can be defended as being rationally acceptable, then theology is allowed a greater range of choice, to its own advantage. Now it is possible to answer the question of this chapter by saying: Philosophy can provide any view required, within reason, that can be defended as one of the possible modes of philosophy.

What philosophy is and can be is perhaps the first of all

theological questions, even for a theology that rejects philosophy. Even an antiphilosophical theology must know what it opposes; and it must be sure it has actually rejected all of philosophy and not merely some one view — or else another view of philosophy will arise to haunt it even if it has argued effectively against one.

Thomas Aquinas needs special attention here as an example, since his view of philosophy is clearly one upon which a complete theology has been built. In that sense, his work stands as a model of what philosophy can and should provide. As an example, then, can Aquinas offer a philosophical basis for contemporary theology? A complete answer to that question would be as long and as detailed as the Thomist doctrines, but briefly we can say: (1) Since any historical view can be revived, so can Thomism, and although (2) Thomism clearly provides the needed basic elements, (3) Thomism, just as clearly, is not the only possible philosophical base. Along with a consideration of Aquinas' doctrine and its value as a model of what ought to be provided, we must now recognize that it is only one possible base. This takes us next to a comparative study of what other foundations can be provided and what advantages or disadvantages each might have in the light of the present theological needs. Our most crucial question here is this: Do we need a philosophy that can help shape a new view of God, and is this where Aquinas and the theological tradition are most in need of revision? In order to further this needed revision of God's nature, we should investigate all the alternative philosophies provided for our examination.

VI *Is Protestantism necessarily antiphilosophical?*

BEFORE GOING BLITHELY on our way under the illusion that we are at last free to form a philosophical basis as needed from a variety of available alternatives, we must pause and consider the question asked by this chapter. For if the answer to it is in any way affirmative, if Protestantism is necessarily anti-philosophical, then we are stopped in our attempt to build a theology that we can call " Protestant " on any philosophical basis whatsoever. It would not be a question of one philosophy being more congenial or helpful than another, but of whether Protestantism, in order to be itself, must somehow reject all philosophies, no matter how harmonious or inharmonious. A serious Protestant cannot treat this issue lightly and proceed to use philosophy theologically, for there is at least some indication of an antiphilosophical temper in the very origins of Protestantism, and this means that the issue cannot be avoided.

Of first concern here is the position that the Biblical documents occupy for most Protestants. Sometimes this is mistakenly identified with a particular doctrine of literal interpretation and verbal accuracy, but these are simply special ways of attempting to stress the fundamental place that sacred Scripture has for Protestants. This Biblical emphasis can become an end in itself, but it should not, since it is a means to accomplish the first aim of Protestantism, as we will outline this below. However, this primary goal does raise special problems for Protestants where philosophy is concerned. These are problems that do not arise in this crucial way for theologies that do not give the Biblical record such a primary place. If the basic statement of religious belief is to be made in technical language, then it is already philosophical, whereas the Scriptural form is in itself clearly not so congenial to philosophical formulation. Paul many times cautions the readers of his letters to beware of entangling the Christian message with vain philosophies.

This is not the place to try out a particular solution to this problem, since that cannot be done short of building a fully developed theology. Yet in trying to build a philosophical base that is congenial to theology, this issue must be raised and the general problem considered. We are in a somewhat better position to do this today, since intensive Biblical study clearly shows that the documents themselves were not free from philosophical influence in the first place. They certainly are not consciously philosophical, nor is it their intent to develop a technical and systematic theology. Still, the influence of certain philosophical modes of the day is clear in the choice of the terms that are used for expressing the Christian announcement in the Bible; this is particularly evident in the variety of images called upon to help express the writer's message. The extent of this philosophical involvement in the formation of the Scriptures is a technical matter for detailed discussion by Biblical experts, but for our question it is important at least to recognize this situation. It means that the Biblical documents cannot be considered as a sure thing, different in kind and completely free from philosophy in their formation.

If philosophy were limited to a single element or else entirely consistent, then the problem might be simpler. Since most of the strains of thought seem to have been borrowed piecemeal and are not systematically developed but represent a variety of forms, we have no choice but continually to seek a more systematic distillation from them. This is separate from the question of whether or not the thought patterns of the New Testament can be directly taken over by later ages. That is a question which rests upon certain views of philosophy and the evolution of thought, and these must not be accepted without philosophical criticism. The point here is that the involvement of philosophy (e.g., in the variety of " names " given to Jesus) makes impossible any treatment of the New Testament documents which would like to exclude all philosophy.

Whether it is possible to recapture in later word forms the exact spirit of the Scripture writers is a question which itself involves philosophical assumptions. A philosophy that says No need not be accepted, but at least with some views, it is not impossible to recapture the spirit without regard to time. How the Scripture is to be approached, then, is not a matter that Scripture itself dictates — at least with a single voice and in terms that do not require interpretation. The mixture of elements in the Biblical documents, a mixture to which the arguments of centuries testify, cannot be easily reduced to one formula without dissent. Such a mixture requires the introduction of philosophy to aid in any systematic rendering, although the extent of philosophy's involvement and the kind of philosophy to be used always remains an open question.

The issue of the relation of philosophy to Biblical interpretation leads to the first item that characterizes the Protestant protest: (1) an attempt to recapture an original spirit, i.e., one that the reformer feels has now become obscured or lost. This being the case, it is easy to see why the Biblical record is always of primary importance for Protestants and why the issue of the involvement of philosophy in Biblical interpretation is a crucial matter. This protest may be one that is directed precisely against the overlay of other theories. These the reformer feels have changed the gospel into something other than itself by imposing alien forms upon it. In such a situation, it is easy to see why all philosophy might be rejected; but in this natural reaction, Protestants must ask whether there can be any Biblical interpretation that is free from all philosophy. If not, then our next question is whether other, more congenial, modes of thought are available in addition to the one protested against as being in need of reform. (That this tendency characterizes Protestantism does not in any way mean that the same spirit is not present in Roman Catholicism.)

As an aside, it should be pointed out that the fundamental role that Scripture fills for Protestants can become, instead of a point of division, a ground for unity with Roman Catholics today. Since it is Roman Catholicism that has sparked reform in this century, perhaps by borrowing from an earlier Protestant reform, it too shares the concern of all reformers to recapture a purity of spirit. Although Scripture cannot play quite the same role for Catholics that it does for Protestants, it can provide a basis for common concern between Protestants and Roman Catholics as Catholics emphasize Scripture in their search for renewal. Unfortunately, today Protestantism must face the charge of often placing an excessive overlay of philosophical views on the Scriptures, so that until Protestants show a similar renewal of interest in recapturing fundamental Scriptural belief, they cannot meet Roman Catholics on the ground that was originally Protestant. In this issue, the question is whether philosophy aids in the recapture of this original spirit or beclouds it. Furthermore, if we are not bound to one philosophy, which form is best and which is worst for attempting to recapture a purity of spirit?

Along with an attempt to recover an original spirit in some purity, Protestantism usually involves (2) a demand for reform in ritual and in practice. The need for this often arises when too wide a separation develops between theory and practice. Then either the theory must be abandoned and made to reflect actual practice, or else current practice must be reformed, if it is judged to be a corruption of the theory. Again we are not attempting to analyze specific instances (e.g., indulgences), but are considering how philosophy is involved. When accumulated ritual grows too heavy and cumbersome and obscures its intent because it cannot point beyond itself, then the Protestant call is for a reform to recapture the purest elements. It demands that ritual be stripped down to essentials in order to get rid of whatever has become a hindrance to the religious life.

In this area again, it is Roman Catholicism that is at the present time most heavily involved in liturgical reform and in a reexamination of practice. Because of the Protestant tendency to deemphasize ritual, it may be that by nature Catholicism calls for a more constant reform here. Still, this move to simplicity and toward earlier forms, as opposed to later additions, is a very real ground for Protestant-Catholic understanding. Where the reform of practice is concerned, however, Protestants may have as far to go as Roman Catholics. Practice has a tendency to move away from theory in every case, so the appearance of this discrepancy is not strange but rather poses a constant problem of reform for every day and for every person.

The question now is how philosophy is involved in this area of reform, that is, whether Protestantism by nature always protests against philosophical involvement in the use of Scripture for the renewal of Christianity. Probably Protestantism's antiphilosophical instinct is basically correct at this point. When ritual and practice need reform it is usually because later and alien ideas have been incorporated; sometimes these ideas have been added without thought as to their effect, but at other times they have been added by the conversion of alien practices which have later slipped back to their original pagan form. This accumulation of thought forms demands continual challenge and reexamination. The irony is that challenging this variety of thought forms a genuine philosophic spirit is opposing a false one. For it is the variety of ideas that is being questioned, although this examination of a variety of assumptions is exactly philosophy's primary function. " Metaphysics " in particular means to examine first principles, to select these consciously, and then to bring all other forms into consistency with them. A reforming age is not antiphilosophical in a basic sense, then, but actually it is highly metaphysical in refusing to accept previous forms without a radical examination of first principles.

Even if a Biblical emphasis is fundamental and a reform of practice need not be basically antiphilosophical but can involve philosophy in its best sense as an ally, there is a third factor related to Protestantism which seems more clearly antiphilosophical. (3) Evangelical zeal is often an aim or a result of reformation. The abuses objected to and the lost spirit which needs to be recaptured hamper the outreach of any religion. One who is already committed to Christianity may not quit even when it is most corrupt and lifeless. He may choose the hard way and stay within it to work for reform. Yet when this is the internal situation, it is difficult to turn all one's energies toward outreach or to preach to non-Christians without reservation and with a clear conscience. Reform must precede any period of powerful outreach, since no one can present a belief to others with conviction if he is not sure about it himself. It is hard for a man to urge very strongly that others join an organization about whose purity and power he himself has doubts.

This perhaps explains the present lack of outer vitality in Christianity while it is involved in a process of soul-searching and inner reconciliation. In any reform movement attention first turns inward — a situation that can be dangerous if the self and the community too long remain the exclusive center of concern. Evangelism cannot be attractive if the outsider is not concerned about internal reorganization and reorientation when this is the major emphasis of the day. But if this process of reorganization is successful and reform once more finds a clear principle to operate by, then evangelism can again be powerful on the basis of an ancient spirit now given a vital contemporary expression.

Philosophy, however, is by nature not interested in preaching and conversion. For the sake of these interests, then, must Protestantism be antiphilosophical? The first thing to be noted is that not all philosophy is alien to evangelical concern. In some of its forms philosophy does have its own way of life to recommend as opposed to religious commitment, but philosophy cannot give total allegiance to any one view or offer any answer as being divinely revealed. In that sense philosophy cannot aid preaching, but does it actually hamper it, so that philosophy must be opposed to the interest of evangelical outreach? First, we must point out that evangelism is usually preceded by a philosophical questioning of assumed forms and by a metaphysical inquiry whose aim it is to establish basic principles clearly. Secondly, forceful preaching requires terms that are well defined, powerful in their meaning for the listeners but nevertheless able to present important and complicated matters simply and yet with accuracy and precision. This is a skill that philosophy has always tried to teach. Such philosophical training is not preaching, but it is a necessary preparation for it. If the message offered involves a confusion of either terms or belief, it cannot be expected to have much effect on the nonbelievers. Philosophical investigation is a prerequisite to powerful proclamation.

In this third area of evangelism, it is interesting to note that neither Protestantism nor Catholicism is ahead of the other. However necessary it may be, ecumenical discussion and reform are still largely an intramural affair; the flowering of our new reforming spirit into evangelical zeal, such as has burst forth to change the scene in some previous eras, has still not yet appeared. In this distilling and discussion stage, philosophy at least in its general spirit of inquiry is both needed and useful. However, when a firm foundation is once again brought into sharp focus, philosophy is not so much needed. Then evangelism will proceed by assuming and using what has previously been clearly defined by the aid of a philosophic skill.

In any attempt to establish how philosophy might aid rather than oppose protest and reformation, we would be blind not to recognize that Protestantism as a matter of fact has tended to adopt antiphilosophical attitudes. This becomes particularly clear when contrasted with the traditional Roman Catholic use of philosophy. Of course, it is precisely this Catholic accommodation to philosophy to which Protestantism has often felt it must object, just as it objected to a decadent scholasticism. Yet if we observe that today it may be Protestant theology that has allowed itself to be determined by certain current philosophical views (e.g., " modern man ") , the role of philosophy becomes much clearer.

It is only a decadent and an unreflective philosophy (i.e., an assumption of forms of thought without basic examination) that Protestantism must object to whenever it feels that this has distorted practice and doctrine. In such cases, as we have pointed out, Protestantism can be seen as a sensitive and a reflective philosophical spirit which protests, as it traditionally does, against an unexamined assumption. But Protestantism's strongest protest today may have to come against its own, now heavily philosophically determined, doctrine. Interestingly enough, in Roman Catholic circles there is rebellion against a dominant scholasticism, although they have preserved that tradition for centuries.

Whenever Protestantism objects primarily to an archaic institutional form or decadent religious practices, then its attitude is practical and it remains neutral as far as philosophy goes. This practical attitude can become antiphilosophical only when the protestor, absorbed in practical battles, turns around to disparage all theory. But Christianity at least cannot long hold this practical attitude, because its history evidences a constant need for a process of theoretical refining.

Nor is this practical outlook post-Biblical, since the theoretical question of Jesus' role and nature were never fully grasped by his disciples. These questions were given clear formulation only after his ministry and not during his lifetime. The debate over Christology is present in the Biblical record itself and is an important issue at the very beginnings of Christianity. We have no idyllic uncontested origin. Christianity required the aid of philosophical reflection from the start, in a way and to an extent which, for example, the Jewish stress on ritual observance does not require. In the New Testament church, as soon as the Holy Spirit had come, the arguments over ecclesiastical procedure and correct doctrine began.

If the aim is always to free the Christian message from distortion, and if Protestants trace some distortion to an excessive philosophical interference, then in that sense Protestantism naturally retains a certain philosophical skepticism. If this is understood and not forgotten, Protestants need not be committed to a rejection of all philosophy. Interestingly enough, this skepticism should incline Protestantism toward nondogmatic forms, i.e., toward philosophical views which internally allow for doctrines other than their own to be " true," rather than to those which claim exclusive truth for themselves. Protestants should not protest against all philosophy but against any monolithic view of philosophy or against the absolute insistence that one procedure is preferable to all others. An openness and a flexibility toward a variety of views would actually seem to fit Protestantism best, but this should never mean an insistence on any one contemporary form to the exclusion of all previous ways of thinking. With Protestantism's primary stress on recovering an original spirit as reflected in the Biblical documents, its most congenial philosophical attitude would be open and pluralistic. This is not because philosophy is the gospel's mortal enemy, but because Protestantism insists on a control over the use of philosophy.

One crucial factor that has changed with the spread of universal education is that philosophical ideas are no longer a force about which only theologians must know and with which only they must deal; now philosophies of all types are everywhere and around us all. This has been true to some extent in other pluralistic and creative times, but with the printing press and universal literacy, philosophical ideas now know no boundaries. Philosophy may be experienced firsthand by every man and not just in secondhand reports. In that sense, then, no clergyman can preach an unphilosophical sermon because his parishioners come to church with a variety of philosophies already on their lips. In such a situation, philosophy cannot be escaped from, even if religion would be simpler if philosophy could be ignored. Although it is probably true that Protestant theology never was free from all philosophical influence, it certainly is not today in any case. It is now necessary to become a philosopher (in spirit at least but not necessarily by endorsing any one doctrine) in order to assess the degree of philosophical intrusion.

Now that it has its own institutions, Protestantism can forget its original protest and can also become too absorbed in institutional matters and in the arrangement of ritual. When this happens, then Protestantism does become antiphilosophical in its practical involvements. Whenever this stage is reached, Protestantism must find its own source of reform. This requires the strength to turn away from an institutional preoccupation in order to return to a stress on its original aim, i.e., to recover the primitive spirit of the gospel. In this situation, Protestantism need not reject philosophy on practical grounds, because it actually needs philosophy in its search for its original first principles, which now may have become obscured.

Sometimes Protestantism has even been antitheological and in this mood it is bound to reject philosophy too. Remembering its original concern for a spirit which had become entangled in unnecessary intellectualism, Protestantism should always be at least a little reserved about technical theology, and it should never let philosophy assume total importance in its life. These reservations seem to require a form of theology that is not dogmatic about the absolute assurance of its own correctness and not a rejection of all forms of theology. Ironically, Protestant theology has often tended toward dogmatics, but perhaps this only represents a failure to understand the implications of its protest. It might merely indicate Protestantism's need for a philosophical spirit that can temper its absolute attachment to any formulation or thought form, including its own.

To put it symbolically, perhaps our trouble as Protestants is that Luther was a priest who rebelled against his superiors and not a layman who rebelled against his priest. In spite of the Protestant spirit of " the priesthood of all believers," Luther could not fail to have a concern for institutional organization and a tendency toward dogmatic formulation. Some forms of Protestantism other than his, it is true, place less emphasis on formal theology, church organization, or ritual practice. But still, beginning as it did, Protestantism was bound to be connected with ecclesiastical concerns.

Protestantism like Roman Catholicism, then, would seem to be in need of lay theologians today. The need is for men who, by virtue of standing outside the hierarchy of the church, are not slanted to its interests, and so are better able to challenge any excessive absorption in ecclesiastical arrangements. Paul was very aware of being a minister of the Christian church and reflects these organizational concerns in ways in which Jesus' preaching does not. We cannot escape Paul's concern for ecclesiastical organization and definition of doctrine, but somehow it needs constantly to be balanced by the detachment from it evidenced in Jesus' message.

It may have taken a priest to challenge a too dominant church, but a second Protestant reformation might well be primarily a lay movement. This would give it a more philosophical cast, since it could not begin as church dogmatics but rather as a challenge to that form of theology as being too church-directed. Not having the institutional church as his primary and necessary interest, a layman is actually better able to turn his concern to those who are outside of his own group, whereas the minister always has primary responsibility for maintaining the institutional form. This of course does not mean that one who is ordained cannot have " a lay attitude," but it is true that he can never forget his responsibility to maintain an institution, unless he is ready to separate himself from it. A lay concern for outreach and an interest in, but detachment from exclusive preoccupation with, an already committed group should characterize Protestantism. These fit a philosophical outlook nicely, whereas church dogmatics tends to fight philosophy, which it sees as a challenge to its self-preoccupation and exclusive claims.

Perhaps one reason for Protestantism's early indifference to philosophy is that, in protesting against abuses and distortions, it could not see at that time that a pure message once recovered would one day itself require defense. Originally, it was hard to visualize that Protestantism would become " ladened with a philosophy" which was uncritically assumed and thus would require philosophical exorcism too. The defense of a message is not the prime consideration in any protest to recover the purity of a message. However, when that message's doctrine is no longer simply accepted, even if presented in a pure form, then philosophy is needed to aid in a critical presentation of what is no longer acceptable in its primitive form. Protestantism began in an era of Christian belief, but, in an age of disbelief, it requires philosophical support to achieve clear form. Although no one philosophy needs to be adopted because of some present temper, as has sometimes been thought to be the case, a nonbelieving age will not pass over discrepancies in the text and unresolved issues without challenging them. Thus, the systematic power of philosophy is required to work out these problems and present the doctrine in a new clear statement.

Whenever a doctrine needs defense, as Christianity now does, neither simple gospel nor practical action, no matter how effective, is enough. A theology must be developed, which means that we need to refine the meaning of the central concepts and then attempt solutions to the difficulties. In this process, philosophy is a necessary ingredient in the development of a theology. A secure age can be theologically indifferent. An age of basic challenge either becomes theological and metaphysical or loses its original belief. Barth's theology meets its opposition by drawing within itself, but that is not an answer to a threat that challenges the very basic assumptions of Christianity itself, unless the opponent is to be converted accidentally. Christian revelation did not announce a self-validating, airtight intellectual system, so to suggest that some one theology is founded exclusively on revelation is to suggest that revelation was more an intellectual event than it was perhaps intended to be (e.g., action vs. words).

Although theologies would seem to be human creations constructed with the aid of philosophy, and therefore prone to all the variability to which the interpretation of words — even God's — are subject, there is nonetheless a basic sense in which any Protestantism should perhaps be antiphilosophical. (4) If the philosophical view employed in theology seems to deny the truth of the message of Christianity (e.g., the resurrection), or if it cannot open direct discussion of God's nature (e.g., by the translation of existential statements about God into statements about man), then this view is of no use to Protestantism. A militant Protestantism, one that is intent upon recovering the purity of the gospel from its accumulated interpretations, should be antiphilosophical. It should not necessarily be against all philosophy, because it should be at least metaphysical enough to ask about the meaning of philosophy itself and then to ask whether or not there is another philosophical view more helpful than the one presently blocking full expression.

We must seek to find out what characterized Protestantism

at its origins, but we must also find out what should characterize it today, now that its original reason for existence has
changed. In the first place, its protesting spirit now must be
directed more against itself than against its mother church.
Such a change in the situation in our era may require a
change in Protestantism's relation to philosophy. In its
present crucial "middle age," it may need to become adept
at the use of comparative philosophy. At its origin it could
assume its context and get by on defining itself in relation to
existent errors and abuses. Now Protestantism must be self-
defined, and that requires more reflection and a basic analysis
of principles. In its youth, it has been antiphilosophical; in
its middle age, it must be philosophically reflective. That is,
it must be able to apply philosophy with caution in order to
achieve its own renewal through the metaphysical exploration of basic assumptions and their effect on the direct expression of the traditional doctrine.

If, ironically, it is Protestantism that is the most dominated
now by questionable philosophical assumptions, then we may
have to appeal to Roman Catholics, in their spirit of renewal,
to reform us too. Although Biblical emphasis has always been
a characteristic of Protestantism, and Protestantism has
stressed Biblical interpretation as fundamental, the interpretation of the Bible has been so heavily colored by various
philosophical approaches that Protestants can no longer rely
on this emphasis if they want to recover an original Christian
message. Due to its centralized control over the formation of
doctrine, Roman Catholic Biblical interpretation often seems
more critical in its relationship to particular philosophical
views, so that the growing emphasis on the Bible in Roman
Catholic circles may be what is needed to hold Protestants to
a Biblically based belief.

It is not that the Bible does not require interpretation nor
that philosophy is not necessary in order to do this; but it
is a question of how to reveal the essential expression of the
message again. We do not mean to beg the question, however,

since the question of what is essential is precisely the challenge and the focus of debate. Once Protestantism stressed the Bible as the norm for the judgment of essentials and rejected any philosophy that seemed to obscure this. Now we witness the irony of Protestantism having become highly philosophical in its Biblical interpretation, after protesting such interpretation earlier. This does not mean that theology is possible without a philosophical basis, but it does seem to imply that, with the rejection of the Biblical witness as the norm, the substitution of a particular philosophical way of thought (e.g., Bultmann's or existentialism) has now determined what is "essential " to belief.

One can almost say that what the radical theologians have done (e.g., Paul van Buren [9]) is to sense the basic philosophy that shapes the Biblical view (in this case Bultmann's) and then to judge that unacceptable. They can do this because to them it is clear that the reinterpretation does not say the same things that the original documents did and because the philosophy involved does not convince them. There is no need to accept any particular philosophical view of course; but when any theology is too closely tied to one philosophy (e.g., Aquinas and Aristotle), a preference for a different philosophical mode (e.g., perfection as not identical with lack of motion and time) tends to force the rejection of all theology along with that philosophy. As argued, this rejection is not a process that can be avoided, that is, if all theology requires some philosophical structure.

Van Buren offers another philosophical framework, in this case British analysis, and then comes up with atheism. In this battle of philosophies (existentialism vs. analysis), one cannot dispense with all philosophy, but no comparative study is made as to the merits and the demerits of all available forms. Barth also proceeds as if one current form of philosophy had no alternative. It is not so much a question of the use of philosophy as it is the unreflective use of one form of it, with no defense made of its virtues over all other forms. If there are inevitably many philosophies and these are considered to be subject to some selection according to purpose, then the Protestant emphasis on the centrality of the Biblical record can survive and even be clarified by a philosophical rendering. It is a characteristic peculiar to Protestantism that it holds the Biblical witness as an independent norm, a norm by which to assess the ability of various interpretations to reveal the source clearly. Then this material is synthesized with metaphysics to yield a theology. *Only a philosophy that claims exclusive right for itself seems to subvert the Protestant Biblical norm, because it allows no norm other than itself.*

Although the first Reformation combined a discontent over conditions in the church with a desire for a radically new spiritual rebirth, our ecumenical decade seems so far to have stressed the former and as yet to have underestimated the latter. Should a new spirit of protest, whether Roman Catholic or Protestant in origin, now direct its attention more toward spiritual rebirth, having begun the institutional reform, would this needed emphasis necessarily be anti-philosophical? If this new spiritual emphasis tends to mysticism, then it might be. But if it looks for a new mode, or for fresh words in which to express a new vitality, then it may turn to philosophy. The religious spirit can never be obvious in its expression; an ability to make it become real through the medium of words will inevitably depend on the philosopher's sensitivity to the intricacies of clear definition and his ability to concentrate meaning in his mastery of the tools of powerful expression.

Does Luther's key discovery of man's justification by faith alone seem to devalue theological study and construction and to make philosophy irrelevant? For any given individual that can personally be the case, as with any intensely personal discovery that forces one away from a domineering thought form; but systematically this requires exposition in order to substantiate the insight. If the insight is new, then old theological formulas, if left intact, may not do justice to its revolutionary power. The forging of new forms of expression or the revival of old ones, whether Biblical or otherwise, is precisely what philosophical skill means. Faith may justify man before God, but that idea itself needs to be justified before man in the form of systematically developed concepts. One cannot put new wine into old wineskins or new thoughts into old concepts without changing them. Is Protestantism antiphilosophical where theology is concerned because the early Protestants launched a tradition of searching Scripture independently of tradition and authority? Again, this may be true for any individual who finds it sufficient, but generally speaking, this tradition works toward philosophy both by demanding a high educational level and by requiring that each man think critically for himself. The Protestant needs to have a philosophically critical mind if he is not to have his belief fashioned for him and if he is himself to take part in its formation. A fixed theological doctrine, as long as it remains unchallenged, can be wedded to only one philosophical form. But both the independent study of Scripture which is inspired by Protestantism and the Bible study which is often its hallmark require philosophical variety and basic flexibility as well as some skill on the part of each individual and not just the professional theologian.

If, regrettably, this flexibility did not exist at first, Protestantism eventually led to the plurality of religious beliefs, to toleration and religious liberty, even if this came only after a period of persecution indulged in by both Roman Catholics and Protestants. Is this ultimate and hard-won result of the Reformation — perhaps a result not even envisaged by the early Reformers in their insistence on one church — a clue to the crucial role that philosophy can play in Protestant theology? If plurality and toleration were not the first goal of the reformers, perhaps their early aversion to philosophical influence in theology was not typical of the role that philosophy eventually came to play in Protestant theology. But that is a theme to develop more fully in the search for a uniquely American Protestant contribution to theology.

VII *Is an American Protestant theology possible?*

Is THE QUESTION of this chapter sheer provincialism in view of the current American drive to be cosmopolitan, to understand all other cultures and their ways sympathetically, and to avoid imposing, as we often have, our mode of life on others? Not necessarily, because in our drive to fit into a sophisticated cultural scene quickly, the trick is that we must understand other ways and other views — as we did not have to do in pioneering or in isolationist days — and still contribute what we might have that is uniquely American.

Our ancestors came from all lands, leaving some inherited ways behind, and yet they preserved much from their earlier modes of thought. As they settled here, they blended this variety into something uniquely American. The political and economic fruits of the new beginning that was achieved in a new land were greatly admired by half the world. Now in a more intellectual era, when the frontiers are gone, it is possible that theology can do today what the constitutional fathers did earlier, that is, bind the independent and the inherited strains together into one union.

Just as America has traditionally been generous in sharing the fruits derived from her special way of life, so also should any proposed American Protestant theology be outgoing, rather than provincial. At least it should not be provincial if it aims beyond home consumption and attempts to form a distinctive theological view that will have wide application elsewhere. In any theological debate, an American theologian ought always to ask himself: What do I have to contribute that is unique, not just a form that I have copied and extended from some other cultural setting? Although he can make good use of these other ways of approaching theology, he should add something to them that can only come from his own background.

The question of what American theology might contribute in this way is the same as asking whether it is intended for universal application or for home consumption. The best products of any age or land, whether Italian painting or Greek philosophy, could only develop out of a people's own circumstances; yet they are not limited to internal use but are free to be used and enjoyed by all. This should be true too of the best American theology (and philosophy), which should come from the American milieu but not be limited to it. The problem is: What can American theology give to the general intellectual scene that others cannot? In our intellectual infancy, we were probably by necessity limited first to copying other forms of thought and then to learning to do them well. We can imitate quite nicely now; but today in our intellectual maturity, we must ask what, if anything, is American theology capable of providing that is unique, rather than an imitation of what was first borrowed?

In the last chapter we asked whether Protestantism by nature must be antiphilosophical where its theology is concerned. In the context of the question of the present chapter, it is possible to give one specific answer to the earlier question. As long as we adopt and carry out imported forms of theology, Protestants need not be philosophical, although there probably is a philosophy already incorporated in their borrowed theology. In order to copy basic forms that are already defined, one does not need to ask philosophical questions. But just as our political forefathers, when they considered breaking with the foreign ruling powers, first had to face the task of defining a basic philosophy for themselves (as a Martin Luther or a Charles Davis must have had to) , so also do we have to face the necessity of becoming metaphysicians in this present theological era. Now we must use philosophy, as we did not have to earlier, in order to work out a basis for theology which is our own and not simply something we have borrowed unreflectively.

The challenges that theology is undergoing today make metaphysicians of us all. We must try to uncover and to examine basic principles that previously could be taken for granted, and then try to work out new first principles that we can express in new ways. The same struggles, of course, are going on in the American political and educational scenes, as an attempt is made to see whether or not old forms can be preserved in a new context. Philosophy becomes a necessity to a Protestant theology that is seeking basic reformulation, if what theology is seeking is not just the extension of an established tradition but the synthesis of an inheritance with a variety of new strains of thought. In such a situation of ferment and radicalism, the careful definition of basic concepts and the molding of a clear intellectual frame of reference become all-important, since no meaning or framework can be assumed to be acceptable to everyone. This search for definitions and principles is philosophy's specific business.

Will a Protestant theology of American origin mean a total break with the European past? No, not unless Americans are really of pure Indian blood. Originally we were strangers and intruders in our own land. We quickly became the descendants of all races and all nations; and as our own traditions are a mixture of almost every tradition, our theology owes something to almost every European intellectual form. Catholicism is strong in America, but it has never been dominant. Jews are perhaps stronger here as a group than anywhere except Israel, and they certainly enjoy a freedom of religious conduct. We inherit all Western — and some Eastern — thought and blood, so that any American theology must first accept that plurality of heritages and then, as a primary aim try to synthesize something unique out of this mixture. To reject outside influence in order to start afresh would actually be to betray our tradition. But, on the other hand, to be dominated by outside influence — especially by any one particular mode of thought that is of external origin — would be to contribute nothing unique to the old world.

A genuine American Protestant theology should be a new, start in a new land, built on a reshaping of old materials for a new purpose. What new purpose does theology in general need today that American thought can provide? Although Jonathan Edwards was an original and powerful American theologian, he comes from an early era in American thought. Today, European theological influences are much more powerful, and the challenges to basic theological premises are also much more radical. Edwards cannot solve our problems, even if he stands as an example of how American theology can develop something new out of old materials.

It might seem strange to suggest at this point that American Protestant thought might provide a fresh concept of God. For at the present time, what we hear most about is a denial of God. Moreover, that denial is based on an inherited concept of the divine nature, a concept that has not been altered but has simply been taken over — and then rejected. This rejection of God is itself the result of a series of imported skepticisms, and thus it cannot even be ruled to be an American contribution. Instead, in denying God we are simply returning in an honest and forthright form that which was first implied, in a less obvious way, by the concepts which were earlier sent to these shores.

Others, more tired of theological labors, can say that God cannot be thought about or grasped in metaphysical terms, but it is the nature of the American spirit to feel that anything can be done and, therefore, not to rule out metaphysics as impossible until it has been tried. Here American courage and willingness to intervene where others have failed should come into play. *The development of a new concept of God in a land that has not yet lost its sense of freshness and youthful vitality should be our theology's aim.*

What distinctive features, then, should American Protestant theology have if it wants to make a unique contribution? We will not attempt to build that theology in detail here, particularly since we will argue that it should have not one form but many. However, we should be able to outline its characteristic features and to relate each to some aspect that is peculiar to the American scene. (1) Our traditional separation of church and state has implications for theology. American theology should not be " church dogmatics "; that is, its primary effort and energy should not go toward working out the structure of the church's life and internal belief. Just as church and state were separated in America, not to harm religion but to protect it from distorting involvements, so should we, in an analogous fashion, direct theology away from a dogmatic institutional form. Theology should be free to be concerned about the life of the spirit and be independent of any institutional interference and involvement.

(2) American democracy was founded on the idea of a balance of powers. We are afraid of too great a concentration of power, and work against it. We balance power between federal and state governments and between the local community and the state; within the Federal Government, we have a balance between the Court, the Congress, and the President. So too theology's health may depend on a variety of religious denominations, philosophies, and theologies, as evidence that no one form of thought is forced upon it. Protestants want no central authority that is capable of becoming dictatorial and suppressing the right of dissent. Americans pay for this freedom in a cumbersome foreign policy and in unruly college students, and theology will pay for it by being unable to offer one theological answer that will exclude all

others; there will be no single, central Protestant voice. Protestants speak only as groups or as individuals, and we are willing to pay the price for such a lack of unified action in religion too.

In an American rush to clear up inefficiency and duplication of effort, business corporations are pushing toward ever-greater mergers in order to meet the demands of an expanding, less fragmented economy, and Protestant denominations too are joining in a form of centralization. Many good results may come from both tendencies, but American Protestantism should still offer freedom from the dictates of any central bureaucracy which the individual conscience cannot accept. Any uniformity of doctrine, or the creation of one large Protestant denomination, is a denial of a heritage that Americans might share with those outside their borders. The drive toward organizational unification is the result of confusion between the real need for spiritual unity of Christians and some supposed need for formal unity of structure to go along with this admirable religious aim.

(3) Only in the American heritage are pluralism in belief and religious tolerance reflected in a pluralism of organizational structure and form. Our government is always the servant of the people; it is elected by them and disposed of by them when it no longer reflects the will of the people it represents. Our way of doing things is not anarchical but pluralistic; we proceed within constitutional limits that do not allow suppression from the top.

Similarly, this pluralism requires a theology which, not only in fact but by its own theory, allows for other theologies and does not claim absolute truth for itself alone. This does not mean taking a theology for granted, as it has seemed to, but rather it involves a constant attempt to formulate new views out of the variety of inherited materials. Communism and Catholicism have always posed special problems in America. We believe in toleration, and so we are forced to tolerate even what might undermine the Constitution or deny the basic principle of pluralism. If Roman Catholicism is moving today toward a pluralistic and democratic base, that is all the more reason for Protestantism to make a virtue out of its present plurality.

In a new era of Christian charity, Catholicism has come to proclaim toleration and a love of the dissenter, a change to be celebrated, but however much it may remove practical obstacles to cooperation and understanding, it does not remove the theological problem. To admit a pluralism of doctrinal base might undermine Catholicism, and yet pluralism is what American Protestants are committed to, however dogmatic Luther may have been in another day and in another land. Does pluralism then require that an American Protestant theology should be unsystematic? No — almost the opposite is true. Americans are known to be highly organized; we are not relaxed about definite procedure but believe every question can be answered openly, given enough energy and effort. Such an attitude has sometimes made us difficult guests in ancient lands, whenever old ways have greater force than speed.

It may be true that pluralism and systematic theology are not incompatible, but is this systematic effort more often applied by Americans only in the practical realms? If so, this would seem to make us ethically oriented, rather than metaphysical. That may have been true in a former era, but it is not true in the sciences today, and it need not be true in theology. Because Americans, if after establishing their independence, became involved for a century or two in the practical problems of opening their frontiers and in developing their lands, does not deny the fact that the country's origin was metaphysical, i.e., that its origins lay in the challenging of long-established assumptions and in the confidence we had in our ability to form and validate new fundamental principles. This challenging of basic assumptions is a theoretical matter, and our science has become great at least partly because of its abstract and pure speculative ability.

(4) If a metaphysical willingness to challenge first principles and to work out new ones and an interest in new systematic effort is genuinely American, these qualities still do not exclude a strong practical drive and involvement and desire to use Christianity to improve the lot of every man. (5) Pragmatism is one of America's few original contributions to philosophy, and in some basic sense it should be an American Protestant theology's base, if not in all details of a single formulation, then at least in basic outlook. Once it was thought that pragmatism was antimetaphysical, but that was because it was anti-Hegelian. Now we see it as simply involving basic assumptions of its own and not as somehow aloof from all metaphysics. As new movements often seem to be, it was more ethically oriented than speculative at its start, and even in its religious forms it did not build new theories about God. But there is no reason why a basic pragmatic spirit might not now be employed in metaphysical construction or be used today to form a new theory of the divine nature.

Our theological needs call for this new theory, and pragmatism does stress a response to the difficulties of the time. If our problems are metaphysical and theological, in the basic sense of the need for a definition of doctrine, then this is where philosophy and theology should direct their energies if they are pragmatically oriented in our day. Speculation is not outlawed, and a divorce of pragmatism from its accidental attachment to empiricism might solve our dilemma. Empiricism seemed at first to be the only way to fight an oppressive philosophical idealism. That battle having been won, it may be that a speculative metaphysics and a new view of God are the pragmatic needs of this day. Not that ethical concern and practical action are ignored, but now their context in basic principles cannot be assumed. Rather, it must first be established before any action can proceed. What we seem to witness in our day is a paralysis of action precisely because every basic principle is under constant question.

It is said that Jesus' era and the Hellenistic age, when Christian doctrine was formed, were both times of wide variation of viewpoints — heterodoxy — and of a multitude of intellectual tongues, i.e., they were ideationally impure eras. If this is so, perhaps such diverse times are the most fruitful if also the most dangerous. (6) Thus, American Protestantism should grow out of both heterodoxy and eclecticism. This need not be a heterodoxy that delights in a confusion of viewpoints or an eclecticism that adds bits and pieces together without an eye to systematic unity. To be helpful, a Protestant theology must be eclectic and build on a heterodoxy of doctrine, but it should do so only with the aim of producing a clear and distinct form. This means a form in terms of which classical questions can be given fresh answers and in which traditional belief is not rejected but is transposed instead into new formulas.

We need to begin by admitting that concepts by definition can never be one; concepts by nature do not allow fixity. When this country began, as is all too clear from our record of Puritanical intolerance and persecution, we did not intend that religious toleration as a principle should lead to a plurality of doctrinal formulas or ritual conduct. Nevertheless, our eventual acceptance of tolerance and religious pluralism of form may have given American Protestantism its unique characteristic. Not only did we flee to America in order to be able to practice a form of worship, but we eventually admitted a variety of forms in addition to the one that the Pilgrims first imported. This leads in a later metaphysical and theological era to the acceptance of heterodoxy and pluralism as basic principles and not as just the historical consequences of rebellion and immigration. Perhaps nowhere is widespread pluralism more a fact than in America; but now we need to make it into a metaphysical principle.

Although America has known its anarchists, this spirit has not been dominant in spite of our tolerance of a pluralism of belief. (7) Actually, a unity of spirit and of action has also characterized our temper. After the process of democratic discussion, we do believe that a Quaker " sense of the meeting " is possible, and we have confidence in our ability to unite in spirit and in action without demanding a conformity of ideas or principles (although some have done this and would confuse democracy by suggesting that it demands a unity of thought too). We promote a variety of ecclesiastical structure and a diversity of intellectual formulation. American stress on action can lead to an assumption that metaphysics and theology are not essential (e.g., in *The Secular City*[10]). Yet our pragmatism should not let us ignore the need to form and reform intellectual principles, especially in a metaphysical era in which so many principles are directly or indirectly challenged.

We need not be dominated by theory, but our love of action can give intellectual formulation its proper place. (8) A basic respect for the individual's right to choose his own principles in the light of his conscience ought to keep us from thinking that our theology is determined for us by forces outside the individual. Our lives and our thoughts may be given their own foundation in basic principles through individual synthesis. American theology ought to appreciate its basic freedom to establish its own theoretical foundations and to have them free from domination by either time or circumstances. This independence does not require a rejection of all imported tradition but simply a sense of being free to shape this tradition in new ways in a new land.

If what theology needs most is a new concept of God, what kind would an American Protestant theology be most likely to produce? Americans often seem to feel old and tired today, so that theologically the problem is to recover the vitality and optimism of our youth. (9) If the vitality of free men lies in their energy to start each day afresh as if they were not burdened by the past, then we should form the picture of a " free " God, one who is capable of starting new each day and not one tired by long historical involvement. It is true that most theologians have attributed "freedom" to their concept of God, but today this must be a freedom based on an ultimate pluralism. It involves a basic flexibility of alternatives in a situation in which intellectual considerations do not dictate a single course of action. A free man accepts the consequences of his actions, and a free God accepts fully responsibility for the form his decisions take.

If variety of intellectual forms and an ultimate pluralism are the basic principles of all things and not just the result of human confusion (i.e., a characteristic of all of Being as well as of man), then this view of a free God is a necessary consequence. In American thought we began by taking the nature of our God for granted, but our recent history no longer recommends that metaphysical luxury. Practically every accepted American concept is under violent attack today, and God is no exception. The American spirit has tried to bring a unity of action out of many varying intellectual views and to do this without demanding their basic conformity. Now we must develop a view of God's nature that is equally amenable to both intellectual variety and clear action. A God not determined from eternity in his course of thought or action should be the contribution of a country that bases its political principles on individual liberty.

Of course, it is one thing to call for such a view of God in general and another thing to provide that systematic concept in metaphysical detail. (I have tried to do this elsewhere, although much more detail remains to be worked out.[11]) The point is not the completeness or the incompleteness of these attempts but the acceptance of the general program of building an American Protestant theology. Should it aim to provide a new view of the nature of God, one built out of the heterodox tradition, but not in opposition to it?

What concept of God in general does our unique tradition and our own time and setting allow us? A freedom of alternatives, an emphasis on choice, a spontaneous ability to begin fresh at every point, and a unity of spirit with no uniformity of doctrine seem to characterize an American temper when it is tied to a stress upon action and results. Theologically speaking, the unique feature of our heritage is our background of pluralism and not our failure to develop a doctrine of God.

We know in advance that any American Protestant theology will yield more than one intellectual system. Its pluralistic base will result in an inevitable pluralism of doctrines, as Catholic theologians have always predicted. Yet it should demonstrate a unity of spirit and action, in spite of its toleration of intellectual diversity, if not actually because of it. This would be a great contribution in itself, even if it cannot establish a single dominant cultural theology. But of course, such unity in the midst of intellectual diversity is not possible in theology without a clear concept of God. The first task of any theology that aims to become a genuine " American Protestant theology " is to provide this concept.

VIII *Can a Protestant theology be Catholic?*

AT FIRST the question of this chapter may seem even more provincial than the question that we asked in Chapter VII. One might admit the possibility of developing a Protestant theology within an American context, a theology which, because of its origins, could contribute something unique. But in an ecumenical era, to speak of a purely Protestant theology may seem to be to take a step in the wrong direction, when what we should seek is a theology, or at least a philosophical base, that will rise above such denominational distinctions. On the other side, one might argue that anything specifically American and Protestant in its origins and in its quality could not, in the nature of the case, be extended to Catholicism or be acceptable for Catholic purposes. At any rate, this question must be faced, especially in a day in which ecumenical concerns have become our preoccupation. Today there is at least the possibility of a search for a common basis, even if it is not possible to work out a single doctrine in detail.

Although this chapter refers specifically to theology, the problem becomes a little easier and perhaps a little clearer if we remember that our basic problem actually concerns the formation of a philosophical *basis* for a contemporary theology, rather than the development of the detailed theology itself. In attempting to outline this philosophical basis in these last chapters, we have tried to see what kind of theology will result from each basis that is selected from philosophy. Thus, the question of this present chapter ultimately goes back to asking how the kind of philosophical base that we are proposing might extend theology to a wider, more catholic use. This question becomes even more crucial when the philosophical base that is selected reflects a specifically American and Protestant context. It could be, of course, that this background is not a hindrance to any theology founded on it, but actually helps to extend the usefulness of that theology, and this problem is what we want to consider.

It has been argued that theology in our era is neither Catholic nor Protestant. This may sound good, but such an argument is really a wishful generosity because it does not hold up in practice. In fact, in an ecumenical era the opposite is true: genuine understanding and a spirit of cooperation depend on facing essential differences, so they do not rise to plague us later, not on ignoring the basic principles about which we differ. Then we can proceed in the light of these differences. If we have anything to contribute to each other, it will be because we have differences and not the opposite, because it will allow all of us to present clearly the unique features of our own thought. In spite of this necessity to face the basic difference over principles, it is possible that the characteristics of the philosophy selected can either help or hinder such communication. How the philosophy used can do this is ultimately the point of this chapter. Can a philosophical base help build a distinctively Protestant and even American theology and at the same time have a definite Catholic application if not appropriation?

Before going any farther here, it must be remembered that the issue, of course, depends on what kind of unity we seek. If we seek a unity of theological doctrine in detail or a unity of ritual practice, the road will be long, and we certainly cannot expect that an acceptable basis for unity can be specifically Protestant or American. More important however, such a view of unity actually rests on a particular conception of philosophy and theology, which holds that we can express essential truth in one set of terms without distortion. Thus, it may be that such unity is neither achievable in principle nor desirable in fact; but without arguing this point in detail, we must ask what other view of unity there might be that could more easily accommodate the inevitable proliferation of forms and ideas and the constant change of ritual. A conception of unity that is put on the theoretical and doctrinal level or that is based on some uniformity of ritual practice might actually be a dangerous aim and lead toward deeper divisions, that is, if such unity cannot be achieved in fact.

On what levels can we seek unity if not on the theoretical level, even if there is still reason to try for greater doctrinal accord whenever possible? Unity on the theological plane may not be possible because theology is an intellectual enterprise that necessarily depends on certain philosophically defined technical terms. Therefore, it is no more subject to finality than philosophy is and no more capable of expressing truth than the frail medium of language is. An attempt to unite on this level would begin an endless quest and perhaps be doomed to produce only deeper divisions in the end. There can be momentary areas of agreement, but theology is a never-ending and an ever-new enterprise. As such it is so susceptible to change and instability and fashion that it is a poor basis for unity. Some people, of course, draw inspiration from the challenge of trying to fix a thought in words so that it can achieve stability. This work is necessary to intellectual clarity and must go on constantly, but it provides a very unstable base for any desired unity.

We should be able to unite without demanding a uniformity of words or agreed-upon definitions. Not that continued attempts at redefinition are unimportant to any group's self-understanding and clear formulation of belief, but definitions define individual groups and precisely for that reason are unsuitable for universal agreement. Any definition can be challenged and any thought can be expressed in different ways, so we should not let unity depend on such a potentially divisive foundation as verbal interpretation. Agreed-on formulas can unite, but because they lack permanence, they can also become a basis for division. It is always possible to disagree with the way something is said and to challenge the technical terms used and the definitions given, since important terms have definite meaning only when specifically defined. We should be able to unite without demanding a unity of words, even if the attempt to overcome differences in formulas must go on constantly.

The primary area of unity might be on the level of a common spirit and a practical application. We need a philosophy to do this that does not take words as being things or as being able to reflect reality directly and without reminder. Differences of form and formulas, then, are not insignificant, but at least they are now seen as secondary. Although we do not expect unity here, we should not allow inevitable differences to stand in our way. If we had unity of spirit, we could meet on an unspoken level and acknowledge a variety of ways in which to express our harmony. This spirit of accord makes agreement on the practical level possible too, since we can go about practical projects without demanding verbal agreement as a condition. Unity seems to be achieved when the differences of formulas are bypassed and an area of spiritual and practical agreement becomes evident prior to the formulas that express them.

As it might appear, this does not mean that every doctrine is to be accepted or that every form of expression is to be taken as equal to every other in clarity and power. Not at all. The intellectual process of continual reformulation goes on and must go on in order to provide clear standards and creeds, but we have simply come to recognize the lack of finality in this process. We do not accept it as primary, however important it may be, and we do not allow it to block a unity of spirit and action. Each form should be distinctive and each formulation must contribute its unique aspects, without expecting a Hegelian synthesis of this process; words and thought do not allow that kind of final summary. Their multiplicity is ultimate, although not chaotic, in God's understanding too. We try for new and ever-clearer formulation, but we do not expect that to provide a basis for unity in itself.

If unity is not placed on the intellectual level of detailed formulas, then we are each free to contribute that which is unique in what we have, without any fear that this will disrupt our unity in any essential way. American Protestantism might ask what it has in its heritage that is not present in any other tradition, and then we should express this in our theology as a contribution to unity, not to division. Our goal, then, is: One spirit but a diversity of theory, one Lord and a common purpose in service to mankind. Depending on the basis that it selects, an American Protestant theology might be very helpful in a movement toward unity, if that unity were able to acknowledge its dependence on a variety and a plurality of form. A proper theology is no respecter of institutional differences, and if its basis does not begin in institutional form, it could allow us to seek a unity of message in spite of differences in practical arrangements. A theology with an acknowledged philosophical form can do this best, because it begins with an independent base and does not depend on the particular arrangements of some institutional form at its point of origin.

Might the qualities of a theology as outlined here provide a basis for unity in spite of differences? They might, if the resulting theology did not claim sole truth for itself. If it makes its formulations as clear and as definite as possible and at the same time maintains in its own theory both openness to alternatives and allowance for new formulations, then such a theology might promote unity rather than further division. This means that any philosophical view that can see no alternatives to its method or its doctrine cannot be the basis for a theology that is conducive to unity. In Chapters IV and V we attempted to list the characteristics needed in theology and in a philosophy which might serve as its base. It is not necessary to repeat these, but in the light of the desire for unity, they must now be appraised to see how, and on what level, each might be able to promote unity, if it is able to do so at all. The claim here, of course, is that these characteristics might promote unity by their nonexclusive approach to truth and by requiring no necessary adherence to one form.

Naturally, Protestants borrowed their message and their doctrine from Catholicism at the outset (or recovered them from within the Christian tradition), and on this base they effected institutional reform. Since it is no longer in that early situation, Protestantism must now work out a theology by establishing a basis developed from within, out of what it has become. Can this new theology also become the basis for reunion, even if institutional differences cannot be overcome? Protestantism's first theology was of necessity a cause of division, but now the situation is quite different for both Protestant and Catholic theology. What we must explore further is whether that group that originally caused division can in a later day find a new basis which, instead of being divisive, might allow for unity, at least in spirit and in practice if not in strict doctrine and institutional structure. When we consider from the Roman Catholic side the main points that prevent a unity of theology, it may be that Protestantism will be able to provide a basis for unity that could not in the nature of the situation come from Roman Catholic sources.

At its origin, Protestant theology could only be built upon a necessity for separation. That being true, how can it now provide a basis for unity? Have times changed that much and in what way? Without attempting to cover the Catholic side adequately, we can say that after the Counter Reformation, which followed the Protestant separation, the two theologies might have been less compatible than at the time of the break. Certain other factors have appeared which hinder unity, as will be mentioned below, but on the other hand the reform and renewal connected with Vatican II make Roman Catholicism more open to reassessment of its theology than perhaps it has been in any recent period. A movement of renewal always has as a part of its process a reaching back to original roots, in an effort to recapture an early freshness of spirit by which to judge whether later additions are distortions of that early message or whether they are helpful expressions.

In Christianity this is bound to involve a Biblical study and emphasis, and since this is an original and fundamental Protestant attitude, renewed Catholic emphasis on the Bible can provide a common meeting ground that will bypass later lines of continuing intellectual and theological divergence. Moreover, given Protestantism's late beginning, any Catholic renewal movement is likely to reemphasize early roots that were common to both prior to their divergence (e.g., the liturgical reforms of the Benedictines, whose origins as an order long antedate Protestant separation). These movements are not in themselves enough to provide theological unity, but they do explain why Catholicism is now in a better position to accept unity than perhaps at any time since the first division. If this is true, if ironically the great impetus for reform in our era has come not directly from Protestants but from the Roman Church, although perhaps by borrowing Protestant materials, why would this same movement not also provide a theological basis for unity? Why should we expect Protestantism to be any more successful here?

Protestantism, as has been argued, is compatible with a doctrine of intellectual pluralism, and thus it can allow at least some, if not all, forms of Christianity to bear a common label. Catholicism, as it has been developed, is not compatible with a pluralism of basic formulation but instead stresses a claim to purity and unity of doctrine. As we have indicated, a search for unity placed on this intellectual basis is hopeless from the beginning, since those who have already experienced the possibility of formulating the same spirit in a variety of ways can never accept a claim to one definitive and infallible formulation, even if it is continually subject to development. If unity cannot be achieved on an intellectual level due to the nature of doctrine and words, and if unity depends on an acceptance of a basic plurality of forms and doctrine, then Roman Catholic thought, despite its present renewal, cannot serve as a basis for unity. Yet a Protestant theology could exist that would include Roman Catholicism, although not with its traditional claims of exclusivity for itself, but simply as one admittedly leading form among others.

If this fundamental difference of outlook on doctrine works to prevent union, what can a Protestant theology hope to contribute to Catholicism? One of the first things it can do is to examine various philosophical bases as to their suitability and point out how certain philosophical assumptions shape the kind of theological doctrine that results.[12] How strange and sad it would be if Protestants and Roman Catholics are separated not so much by differences over an understanding of the fundamentals of Christianity (as it may have been at first), but rather by certain philosophical views about the nature and status of theological doctrines! Catholicism has always been more philosophically conscious than Protestantism, but if Catholicism has wrongly understood the singularity of philosophy or the kind of certainty that any verbal formulation may have, then perhaps a Protestant philosophical inquiry might be helpful. Protestantism can point out the plurality of possible philosophical forms and the impossibility of ever establishing one form as superior in all respects or as free from alternatives.

The way in which "the church" and the function of its hierarchy are understood will probably always divide Protestants from Catholics; for Protestants at least hope that we will never move toward a single institutional form. On this point Protestant theology is again more amenable to unity than Catholic thought, in that it can accept a variety of institutional forms and concepts and can tolerate a diversity of form which Catholicism has not so far seemed able to do. In this way Protestantism can accept Catholicism as a genuine form of Christianity in ways in which Catholics (barring a revolution) could never accept Protestantism, with its variety of forms each viewing the role of its leadership differently. Roman Catholics cannot accept this variety as a basis for unity, since pluralism is incompatible with their understanding of Catholic doctrine, but it is apparent that a Protestant basis for unity can allow Catholicism to be true in ways in which Catholicism can never accept Protestant doctrine, that is, unless the post-Vatican II debate succeeds in forcing a further revision of basic doctrine.

If there are fundamental features of Roman Catholicism that prevent it from serving as a basis for a pluralistic unity and ways in which a Protestant theology can promote this, how can a philosophical basis help when other approaches to Protestant theology might not? If Protestant theology builds only on its various views of the church, or upon its doctrinal or liturgical past, these issues will further accentuate our differences in form, however much they might be brought close to Catholic practice at points.

A philosophical approach to theology, if critically appraised, can be a neutral basis. It can avoid, in its principles at least, a long history of intricate and involved differences. Perhaps a new basis of interpretation, bypassing old and entrenched differences over terms, might be found that could provide fresh formulas acceptable to all, since one cannot completely resolve arguments that have been ingrained over centuries. The usefulness of such an approach also depends on the ability of that philosophical basis to allow full expression of the essential Christian message. Otherwise no unity is possible, and that philosophical view itself becomes simply a further item of contention.

A common Biblical emphasis is, of course, important here, but if a theology cannot be built from Biblical texts without the aid of some philosophical structure, then focusing attention on the Bible will not in itself bring unity. Everything depends on how the theology is formulated from that point on, and we know that the Biblical texts themselves contain a variety of philosophical forms. Because these forms do not represent doctrinal purity, systematic work is required in order to reconcile the various modes of interpretation that are present within the texts as different ways of revealing one theme. It is true that we can still find some technical terms for theology which refer more toward the Biblical text than other sources, and in that sense a Biblical point of reference might serve to unify, even if the technical theologies elaborated from the texts cannot.

A philosophical base can promote unity if it does not claim an exclusive right for its doctrine, but this, as we have noted, is a prime area of contention. It can also help promote unity if the philosophical base is nonhistorical in its emphasis, for then it tends not to demand a reconciliation of all past doctrinal divergence as a condition for a present basis of unity. If historical thought could yield one interpretation, one logical process, and be seen as a single line of development, then a unity might be possible. But if a historical orientation not only cannot yield this unity but instead makes divisions deeper, then a nonhistorical philosophy is more helpful to unity because it will bypass entrenched divisions in an attempt to find a fresh beginning. What we seek is not a totally new view but a view refreshed by a direct return to its original common source. Unity can only be sought on the basis of a core of central belief from which specific details are separated, but here again a clear basis is needed to assess what is and what is not central.

The philosophical foundation that has been suggested here does not betray its own principles. That is, it does not take itself as being final or exclusive, even in the terms and concepts that it uses. Philosophy is " one thing " in the questions that it asks, but it is never one in its use of terms, or in the specific ways in which the questions are dealt with, or in the answers formulated. Such a philosophical base does not demand conformity to its particular mode of expression as the price for cooperation. Any artificial rigidity and certainty of formulas is a block to unity, because not everyone can accept them. A basis like this could admit Catholicism because it allows for development in a number of ways, but this variety is not acceptable at present to the philosophical basis that supports Roman Catholicism. Yet a critique that calls attention to the fact that the basic disagreement really is over philosophy (i.e., over how one understands the fixity and the finality of any verbal formulation) might promote unity by pointing out where the issue lies.

We began by trying to state what kind of philosophy we need, and then in the light of this, we examined the present theological scene and the available philosophic sources. We tried to state briefly what we need for a theology and what kind of philosophy we should have. One major problem is the antiphilosophical tendency that seems to have characterized Protestant theology. Then we asked what a genuine American Protestant theology might contribute and how it could be useful in achieving a unity with Roman Catholicism. It is clear that Protestantism has tended to become antiphilosophical (and may even have begun that way) because it is philosophy that divides us. It is not a basic understanding of the original Christian events that is at issue, but how they are to be expressed and what theoretical concepts are to be used in this process.

Now that an openness of spirit and a desire for renewal have swept Catholicism, it is clearer than ever that the basic disagreement is essentially the result of philosophical differences. That is, no one can speak infallibly unless his supporting philosophy can conceive of words bearing the weight of this burden. A singleness of interpretation and formulation and a denial of pluralistic form are dependent on a philosophical view that allows such unity. But how is that particular philosophical view to be validated among its competitors?

No view of the development or evolution of doctrine can ever be central to the belief of Christians, since evolutionary doctrine is simply one debatable approach to Christian belief by way of a certain philosophical interpretation.

In a day when Catholicism stresses renewal and reform and has agreed to a reappraisal of the Biblical foundations of belief, Protestant theologians do not seem to have a version of orthodoxy to contribute to the discussion, and even their spiritual vitality has weakened. What they might contribute today is what they once fought against, namely, a clear philosophical basis for theology. This philosophy cannot be offered as the single best basis for theology. If a critical reappraisal of every philosophical basis is possible, it might help in understanding the importance of doctrine if the philosophical issues dividing Catholics and Protestants (and perhaps dividing Catholics too) were highlighted. *A new philosophical base for Protestant theology should make clear how any Catholic philosophical assumption stands as merely one among many possible philosophical modes and why this mode cannot be assumed by theology but instead demands prior philosophical justification.*

It makes a great deal of difference, in fact, it makes all the difference in the world, how one understands the status that any doctrinal formulation can have. What kind of knowledge a mind can hope to have and the meaning to be given to revelation are questions not determined in advance but which can only be worked out individually and afresh in every age. Most important, what can be known about God, and how it can be known, is not specified in detail in Scripture but finds its place in tradition only after philosophical interpretation. If God were easily discernible, perhaps theology might not be so dependent on philosophy. But the variety of ways in which God has been described, even within the Christian tradition, manifests the work of many philosophical views more than any action on God's part to define his nature for us. If God intended such definition to be a part of revelation, then we would have to pronounce his attempt rather unsuccessful in view of the infinite variety of interpretations that resulted, or at least we would have to say that his self-disclosure is compatible with a pluralism of formulas.

If any one philosophy, whether based on skepticism or on mysticism, restricts or denies our ability to conceive of or to talk about God, this restriction is almost more important than the variety of ways of conceiving of God, and it is an issue that demands prior attention. Since this issue is a matter of philosophy, it appears that present-day Protestantism, perhaps not realizing it, has the root of its differences with Catholicism in such a philosophical problem. Some current philosophies that shape Protestant theology are probably unacceptable to Catholicism because they do not allow a full expression of Christian claims. In this case, the greatest service Protestantism can render to the cause of unity is to conduct a thorough reexamination of its present philosophical base and of all other possible philosophical bases.

Then, in highlighting its differences with Roman Catholicism over matters of philosophy, Protestantism might point out by contrast the kinds of philosophical principles that go into shaping Roman Catholic thought. In that sense a Protestant theology could be Catholic — by placing the emphasis where it belongs — not on a difference about Christianity but in a disagreement over the best philosophical basis for its present interpretation and what that base will and will not allow us to say.

CONCLUDING POSTSCRIPT

IF WE WANT TO WORK to secure the future of theology, how shall we begin and how can we measure our success? The answer to the last question is, of course, " May the best man win." In a creative and upsetting time such as this, many suggestions and attempts will be made. In an open and pluralistic society, the only control we have over doctrine is to see what works its way into practice and ingrains itself into the tradition. Roman Catholic procedures for effecting these changes are more elaborate and more clear-cut, but still, in an age in which Catholics are also willing to receive suggestions from every source, Protestant theology has an obligation to work to keep all sources open and to pursue every constructive possibility.

Most of all, we need to proceed with philosophical caution. That is, we must examine carefully and critically every suggested philosophical theory to be quite sure that philosophical pronouncements do not stand in the way of our potential unity over the gospel. This is as much true of Biblical interpretation as of other areas, so that our major need seems to be to become metaphysicians. This means to work backward to appraise assumptions first, rather than to accept terminology and our theoretical context and simply to work forward. The hidden philosophical assumptions in theological

procedure may very well be our chief source of division today, and to appraise these we must all become metaphysicians
whose first concern is with first principles. If a wide source
and variety of philosophical contexts are now open to us,
then we have more theoretical freedom today; but the task
is also more difficult, just because our conceptual structure
is not given to us but must be made by us.

In a time when every American tradition is under attack,
it may seem strange to our ears to hear a call for an " American " Protestant theology. Today we seem sick of national
boundaries and of everything that divides men, and perhaps
never before have we raised a younger generation so disen-
chanted with America or so little likely to respond to patriotic
appeals. Yet, precisely for that reason, it might be worth-
while to see what of theological value the American tradition can produce. For if our restlessness is about our present
policy, then perhaps the best way to understand America is
not to see her in her present confusion but to recover from
the past a note that we think more genuinely American in
its tone.

However, Kierkegaard warned us in his *Philosophical
Fragments* that to look back to the fixity of the past and to
take refuge in historical certainty is a false security. The future remains to be worked out, and it is full of both uncertainty and freedom. The appeal to past glories has lost its
appeal today, but perhaps this only means that the American
tradition must first be rediscovered and then transformed
into a form suitable to the future. To do this might be the
best tribute we could pay to our past heroes.

If America is torn by self-doubt, as perhaps it has been at
no time since the Civil War, theology today is equally in a
state of turmoil. Such conditions form a potentially creative
situation, but the possibilities for total disintegration and
loss of tradition also run high. Our theology is little likely to
solve our political and international dilemmas, it is true, but
at least we might try to recover the best in the American

tradition and then use it to speak as forcefully to the present as we can.

In his *Philosophical Fragments*, Kierkegaard did something like what is needed today. He took the central issues of Christian doctrine and set them in a fresh philosophical form. With the aid of the leverage of this new context, he was able to reinterpret the " good news " of Jesus' life and work in ways that a new generation might appropriate effectively. Our churches have recently come to life again, and perhaps also into crisis, over current racial and social issues and over the ancient moral dilemma of war. It may be that we cannot solve these questions religiously today. But our present *crisis of faith* might at least cause us to look back to the original Christian message, to overcome the divisions of centuries, to criticize and to remove philosophical interpretations that need not be there, and then to seek not one new form but several current forms within which the ancient doctrine can be made contemporary.

Our questions today are so basic, so involved with first principles rather than detail, that theological doctrine must wait for a prior metaphysical exploration and for a philosophical investigation of first principles. Our questions go beneath the level of theological doctrine, and we cannot settle our differences on that level until we have first agreed on the philosophical base or bases open to us. This is a difficult situation for theologians who would rather work out the fine points than debate basic structure. Just how much contemporary philosophy is in a position to help us in either the political or the theological debate, this is a very questionable matter. It would be nice to have a ready-made philosophical context in such a time of upheaval, but, lacking this, our age may yet make constructive and critical metaphysicians of us all. Whatever our reservations about metaphysics may be, the crisis of the hour does not seem to leave us any other choice but to begin with a critical examination and comparison of the alternative sets of first principles open to our use.

NOTES

1. See my book *The God of Atheism: An Argument from the Existence of the Devil* (Doubleday & Company, Inc., 1969).

2. John Macquarrie, *Twentieth-Century Religious Thought: The Frontiers of Philosophy and Theology, 1900–1960* (Harper & Row, Publishers, Inc., 1963). All page references that follow are to this volume.

3. See my book *The Existentialist Prolegomena: To a Future Metaphysics* (The University of Chicago Press, 1968).

4. For an explanation of how metaphysics operates, see my book *The Problems of Metaphysics* (Chandler Publishing Co., 1968).

5. For a critical defense of this new basis for metaphysics, see my book *The Existentalist Prolegomena: To a Future Metaphysics.*

6. *Ibid.*

7. For an attempted reconciliation, see my book *Divine Perfection: Possible Ideas of God* (Harper & Row, Publishers, Inc., 1962). Also published by SCM Press, Ltd., in the Library of Philosophy and Theology (London, 1962).

8. *The Existentialist Prolegomena: To a Future Metaphysics* based on psychological and literary insight.

9. Paul van Buren, *The Secular Meaning of the Gospel* (The Macmillan Company, 1963).

10. Harvey Cox, *The Secular City* (The Macmillan Company, 1965).

11. *Divine Perfection: Possible Ideas of God* and *The Existentialist Prolegomena: To a Future Metaphysics.*

12. For a further analysis of the relation between philosophy and theology, see my book *How Philosophy Shapes Theology: Problems in the Philosophy of Religion* (Harper & Row, Publishers, Inc., forthcoming).

SELECTED BIBLIOGRAPHY

Altizer, Thomas J. J., *The Gospel of Christian Atheism*. The Westminster Press, 1966.
———— and Hamilton, William, *Radical Theology and the Death of God*. The Bobbs-Merrill Company, Inc., 1966.
Barth, Karl, *Church Dogmatics I: The Doctrine of the Word of God*, Part 1, tr. by G. T. Thomson. Edinburgh: T. & T. Clark, 1936.
———— *The Knowledge of God and the Service of God*, tr. by J. L. M. Haire and Ian Henderson. London: Hodder & Stoughton, Ltd., 1938.
Bergson, Henri, *Creative Evolution*, tr. by Arthur Mitchell. Modern Library, Inc., 1944.
Bonhoeffer, Dietrich, *Ethics*, ed. by Eberhard Bethge, tr. by N. H. Smith (The Fontana Library). London: William Collins Sons & Co., Ltd., 1964.
———— *Letters and Papers from Prison*, ed. by Eberhard Bethge, tr. by Reginald H. Fuller. The Macmillan Company, 1953.
Bultmann, Rudolf, *Theology of the New Testament*, tr. by Kendrick Grobel. 2 vols. London: SCM Press, Ltd., 1952, 1955.
Christian, William A., *Meaning and Truth in Religion*. Princeton University Press, 1964.
Cobb, John B., Jr., *A Christian Natural Theology*. The Westminster Press, 1965.
Cox, Harvey, *The Secular City*. The Macmillan Company, 1965.
Dewey, John, *A Common Faith*. Yale University Press, 1934.
Hamilton, William, *The New Essence of Christianity*. Association Press, 1961.
Hartshorne, Charles, *The Divine Relativity: A Social Conception of God*. Yale University Press, 1948.

Heidegger, Martin, *Being and Time,* tr. by John Macquarrie and Edward Robinson. London: SCM Press, Ltd., 1962.

Hocking, William Ernest, *The Meaning of God in Human Experience.* Yale University Press, 1912.

Husserl, Edmund, *Ideas: General Introduction to Pure Phenomenology,* tr. by W. R. Boyce Gibson. The Macmillan Company, 1931.

James, William, *Pragmatism.* Longmans, Green & Company, Inc., 1948.

Kierkegaard, Søren, *Concluding Unscientific Postscript,* tr. by David F. Swenson and Walter Lowrie. Princeton University Press, 1941.

—— *Philosophical Fragments,* tr. by David F. Swenson. Princeton University Press, 1936.

Macquarrie, John, *An Existentialist Theology.* The Macmillan Company, 1955.

—— *God-Talk.* London: SCM Press, Ltd., 1967.

—— *Twentieth-Century Religious Thought: The Frontiers of Philosophy and Theology, 1900–1960.* Harper & Row, Publishers, Inc., 1963.

Mascall, E. L., *The Secularization of Christianity.* London: Darton, Longman & Todd, Ltd., 1965.

Niebuhr, Reinhold, *The Nature and Destiny of Man.* Charles Scribner's Sons, 1948.

Ogden, Schubert, *Christ Without Myth.* Harper & Row, Publishers, Inc., 1961.

Ramsey, Ian T., *Religious Language.* London: SCM Press, Ltd., 1957.

Roth, Robert J., S.J., *American Religious Philosophy.* Harcourt, Brace and World, Inc., 1967.

Royce, Josiah, *The Religious Aspect of Philosophy.* Harper & Brothers, 1958.

Sartre, Jean-Paul, *Being and Nothingness,* tr. by Hazel Barnes. Philosophical Library, Inc., 1956.

Sontag, Frederick, *The Crisis of Faith: A Protestant Witness in Rome.* Doubleday & Company, Inc., 1969.

—— *Divine Perfection: Possible Ideas of God.* Harper & Row, Publishers, Inc., 1962. Also published in the Library of Philosophy and Theology. London: SCM Press, Ltd., 1962.

—— *The Existentialist Prolegomena: To a Future Metaphysics.* The University of Chicago Press, 1968.

—— *The God of Atheism: An Argument from the Existence of the Devil.* Doubleday & Company, Inc., 1969.

—— *How Philosophy Shapes Theology: Problems in the Philosophy of Religion.* Harper & Row, Publishers, Inc., forthcoming.

—— *The Problems of Metaphysics.* Chandler Publishing Co., 1969.

Tillich, Paul, *Systematic Theology.* The University of Chicago Press, 1951–1963. 3 vols.

Van Buren, Paul, *The Secular Meaning of the Gospel.* London: SCM Press, Ltd., 1963.

Weiss, Paul, *The God We Seek.* Southern Illinois University Press, 1964.

Whitehead, Alfred North, *Process and Reality.* The Macmillan Company, 1929.

Wittgenstein, Ludwig, *Philosophical Investigations,* tr. by G. E. R. Anscombe. The Macmillan Company, 1961.